I0441836

CONTENTS

INTRODUCTION: BUILDING A CONTEXT FOR ANALYSIS

From time to time in American history, the limits of executive branch secrecy have been questioned in what has occasionally become impassioned debate. We may find the level of secrecy held by the executive and the amount of information received by the Congress to rest in a balance. Quite often, heated debate over the status quo of this balance has led to momentous shifts in favor of one branch or the other. The nature of the changes in this balance will become the focal point of this investigation.

Scholars and public officials have often tried to pinpoint an exact position where the balance of secrecy should ideally rest. Those who support the executive branch's right to withhold information have most often claimed national security as the primary basis for denying disclosure. Critics who favor greater openness between the executive and the Congress use the Constitution and legal citations as the center of their argument. Numerous policy options have been suggested in order to permanently assign a unalterable position for this balance. When these arguments are fully considered in the context of history, we find that they fail to weigh the strongest force which acts upon the balance of secrecy. The overriding element in this struggle is political power. The most effective way of proving this assertion is first to disprove the validity of the most

commonly stated justifications for altering the level of
secrecy.

National security as well as legal arguments may
serve as explanations which could shift public support in
favor of one branch or the other. However, careful
consideration of these and other justifications proves that
such arguments bear little relevance to the final position
of the secrecy balance. In most cases, an information
release to Congress represents only a minuscule threat to
national security. Legal citations invoked in support of
Congress' right to information carry little penalty for
noncompliance. Once these and other nonessential grounds
for shifting the balance are pushed aside, secrecy may be
properly viewed as a contentious battle for power.

Once auxiliary components of the struggle over
secrecy are set aside, an investigation of this balance may
be conducted on two principal levels. The first level of
analysis will revolve around the results of secrecy on the
overall balance of power in the political arena. Once we
prove that secrecy is a significant element of power in
national government, we must then address how this element
may be adjusted. This adjustment forms the basis for the
second level of analysis which consists of an examination of
a number of means by which the balance of secrecy may be
altered.

In March of 1983, President Reagan called for the

commencement of a research program promising to eventually create a strategic shift in U.S. national security policy. In the ten years following its inception, the Strategic Defense Initiative (SDI) has become one of the today's most controversial weapon systems. The intense level of debate, the strong interest of both Congress and the executive branch, and the high level of secrecy surrounding this project make it an ideal case study for this investigation.

The question of secrecy requires an examination of law, politics and decision making. When examined in the context of defense information, the question evolves into one which includes elements of national security and international relations. When the focus of this study is narrowed to the case study of SDI, considerations of the complex area of arms control must be incorporated into the discussion. This study will assimilate research conducted across these and other relevant areas of analysis in order to synthesize a conclusion which is both pragmatic and rational. Failure to fully consider each of these related fields in the past has often led scholars to disproportionately accentuate singular elements of this struggle.

EXECUTIVE JUSTIFICATIONS FOR WITHHOLDING INFORMATION

The National Security Argument

When the executive branch of government chooses to withhold defense information, justification is most often made on the grounds of national security. The term "national security", however, has always been viewed as one which holds a very wide definition. For example, the National Security Council was created in 1947 in an attempt "to facilitate intragovernmental coordination, especially between the Department of Defense and the State Department."[1] According to the United States Code, "National Defense" is defined as, "A generic concept of broad connotations and referred to the military and naval establishments and the related activities of national preparedness."[2]

Common political discourse often uses the term very broadly as one of the most popular justifications for refusing to produce classified material. In 1807, Thomas Jefferson received a letter from General Wilkinson which contained certain "state secrets." He later chose to, "Withhold communication of any parts of the letter which are

---

[1]   Robert L. Pfaltzgraff and Jacquelyn K. Davis, National Security Decisions: The Participants Speak (Lexington, Massachusetts: Lexington Books, 1990), 1.

[2]   18 U.S.C., Sec. 793, Note 5 (1941).

not directly material for the purposes of justice," on the basis of "national safety."[3] Almost 200 years later, the courts have not yet settled on any one definition for checking a government claim of a "national security threat."[4]

While the term "national security" is extremely vague, certain specific components of this concept directly relate to government restrictions on information. Within national security's sub-field of foreign affairs, the maintenance of strict limitations on information access protects the trust of both our allies and opponents during delicate international negotiations. From a military perspective, keeping a tight hold on information allows us to preserve our technological lead in the arms race and prevent the proliferation of weapons to unapproved nations. Furthermore, secrecy facilitates the United States' ability to maintain the initiative and implement the element of surprise during times of conflict. These and other elements of the wide sphere of national security might be referred to as distinctive reasons for withholding information. In order to determine whether national security is a sufficient justification for withholding information, we must address

---

[3] Raoul Berger, Executive Privilege: A Constitutional Myth (Cambridge, Massachusetts: Harvard University Press, 1974), 188.

[4] Ellit E. Maxwell, "The CIA's Secret Funding and the Constitution," Yale Law Journal 84 (1975): 627.

each of its relevant elements.

The Element of Foreign Affairs
in the National Security Argument

Some foreign policy experts, such as former
Secretary of State Henry Kissinger, often cite international
relations as a main reason for maintaining rigid
restrictions on classified information. When the precedent
of the Cold War is examined, this argument is found to be
quite plausible. Secrecy has continually been used as an
instrument which allows the executive to maintain positive
control over who receives certain technology. The use of
such techniques requires policy makers to act
conscientiously and in a timely manner.

Some scientists, such as Edward Teller of Stanford
University, strongly disagree with this argument. It is
Teller's opinion that keeping defense technology information
secret hinders U.S. relations with its allies.[5] According
to this logic, secrecy might prevent friendly nations from
capitalizing on the research and development of the United
States. First, the fiscal barrier of research and
development might prevent that nation from participating in

---

5 Greg Schmergel, ed., U.S. Foreign Policy in the
1990's (New York: Saint Martin's Press, 1991), 223.

collective security. Second, any money which that nation does allocate towards military production will be spent on procuring weapons that are less than state-of-the-art. These impediments would not only cause others to view us in a negative light, but they also hinder the military strength of these nations. If the United States later chooses to form a military coalition, as it did in the Persian Gulf War, the collective strength of the group will be thereby reduced. Worse yet, the United States' failure to cooperate with information exchanges might lead a nation to refrain from participating in such a conflict.

If the United States did not share defense technology with its allies, arguments such as Teller's would indeed hold true. However, a security classification does not necessarily represent a lack of cooperation. Indiscriminate declassification of defense information would limit the United States' means of positively controlling the forces which shape international security conditions. The United States maintains massive power in the sophisticated weapons technology which it holds. To leave such power unchecked by exposing it the entire world would be highly contemptible.

In some ways, it is true that the refusal to release information regarding defense technology may be detrimental to our relations with our allies. However, the major implications which such release may carry with it make it essential that the information disclosure be strictly controlled. Proponents of secrecy would claim that this control must be maintained within the U.S. government as well as on an international level. Strict regulations on information access within a government is seen as a method of preventing that information from being leaked.[6]

When information is leaked by other than official sources, the act may undermine the overall integrity of an administration's policy. An information release on an unauthorized basis represents the waste of a valuable political commodity. The United States might have capitalized on the intrinsic value of this information had the release been undertaken through official channels. For example, the United States might have chosen to deliver this information to an ally in exchange for certain concessions made by that nation. These concepts have been made particularly clear by the experiences of the United States in the nuclear arms race.

Throughout the Cold War era, the United States used secrecy in different methods and in varying degrees to keep a strategic advantage over the rest of the world in the area of nuclear weapons. From the time of the Manhattan District Project until 1949, the aim of secrecy was to preserve the U.S. monopoly. After the first Soviet atomic detonation in

---

[6] The official definition of the word leak is, "To give out information surreptitiously." In almost every case, such actions are carried out for political purposes.

1949, the focus shifted toward preventing the Russians from overtaking the U.S. (although keeping the information from the rest of the world was the second highest priority).

A reversal of this policy was seen between 1953 and 1960. Under Eisenhower, Russia was no longer the primary focus of nuclear secrecy. Instead, information restrictions were aimed at China, continental allies in Europe, and all other nations which sought a nuclear capability. Although Britain first made significant advances in its nuclear weapons program in 1952, the United States did not choose to collaborate fully with that nation until 1958.[7] During this era, the United States was not the only nation which followed a careful process of withholding and releasing information with its allies. Quite similarly, the Soviets strategically gave secret technological data to Warsaw Pact countries and other allies throughout this and other periods of the Cold War.

In 1957, Henry Kissinger harshly criticized this policy of keeping nuclear secrets from the continental allies in his book, Nuclear Weapons and Foreign Policy. He feared that the allies were, "Assailed by a sense of impotence and [could] fall easy prey to Soviet propaganda,"[8] during this fleeting period of secrecy. He

[7]   Harold L. Nieburg, Nuclear Secrecy and Foreign Policy (Washington: Public Affairs Press, 1964), 17.

[8]   Henry A. Kissinger, Nuclear Weapons and Foreign Policy (New York: Harper & Brothers, 1957), 311.

believed that the current policy could not be sustained indefinitely if the United States hoped to maintain the alliance. This realist view of the situation stood at odds with the opinions of other experts of the time who favored controlling the production of arms by all means possible.[9]

If a member of Congress were to concur with Kissinger's disagreement with the administration's policy, that member would be placed in a complex situation. On one hand, he would have an obligation to correct the problem. As a member of Congress, one might have access to some of the technical data which an ally would need to begin its own nuclear weapons program. Any information which such an individual could leak from Capitol Hill could become an instrument used in moving toward a revision of such policy.

On the other hand, a member would be constrained by the information restrictions imposed by an administration which that member considered faulty in judgement. If that member were to view this situation in such a context, the representative might consider an unapproved disclosure to be a brave, patriotic endeavor. The end result would be a legislative version of the Iran-Contra Affair. In both this example and Iran-Contra, unauthorized actions were made outside the boundaries of the law in attempts to achieve

---

[9]   Kissinger evaluated The Price of Peace: A Plan for Disarmament, by Charles Bolte as being, "A passionate plea for disarmament...marred by a...total unconcern with technical and political problems." [Kissinger, 447]

some end which the participants found to be morally justifiable.

Restricting Congress from making deals with other nations does not negate its role in foreign policy. For example, delicate international agreements made by members of the executive branch may be rendered powerless if they are not approved by the Congress. When the issue of secrecy is considered from the perspective of the legislative branch in a later section, these powers of the Congress will be thoroughly enumerated.

Henry Kissinger once again considered the intricacies of secrecy as an adviser to President Nixon. While conducting delicate negotiations with China in 1971, the Pentagon Papers were released by Pentagon-insider Daniel Ellsberg. These documents, which contained a classified history of the Vietnam War, created a national embarrassment.[10] What resulted was an excellent example of the complexities which are brought about by government secrecy. Kissinger feared that this embarrassing disclosure of national security secrets might undermine U.S. credibility and ruin the negotiations he had planned for a covert trip to Beijing on July 1.[11]

---

[10] Michael Schudson, Watergate in American Memory: How We Remember, Forget, and Reconstruct the Past (New York: Basic Books, 1992), 18.

[11] Walter Isaacson, Kissinger: A Biography (New York: Simon and Schuster, 1992), 331.

Kissinger's change in perspective regarding the issue of information declassificaticn demonstrated the ambiguous nature of the concept of national security as it relates to secrecy. As a senior government official, Kissinger would repeatedly claim national security as the main reason for withholding information from Congress. The comparison between Kissinger's viewpoints on these two separate issue is not made to demonstrate inconsistency on his part. In fact, each example exhibits attempts at absolute and dynamic executive control over classified information. Instead, they show how withholding and releasing information may be shrewdly conducted to maximize the productivity of the executive branch. In addition, Kissinger's change in perspective might be seen as a proof of the adage, "Where one stands depends on where one sits." From the outside, Kissinger critiqued the problems created by government secrecy. Later, as a cabinet level official, he found secrecy to be a potent political tool.

The Parallel Between International Relations and Technology Development:

An analysis of government non-disclosure in the area of foreign affai:· provides valuable insight into the advantages and disadvantages of secrecy. A constructive parallel might be drawn between international negotiations and defense research and development. If either of these processes is frequently brought under intense congressional scrutiny throughout their preliminary stages, unjust measures could be taken to hinder advances in their activity. Minor setbacks might be exploited as failures of the entire program. Such misperceptions might be used by members of Congress as a means of convincing their colleagues that funding should be reduced or that the program should be terminated.

However, when the national security policy-making process is viewed from a broad perspective, a critical difference is seen between secrecy in international relations and secrecy concerning classified defense technology. Many scholars have taken a Machiavellian view of international relations. As Robert A. Dahl once observed,

> The bargaining conference ought to be subsidiary
> to basic policy. And it is the latter, not the
> process of negotiation, that ought to be set by
> open and public debate.[12]

In international relations, the means are most often held

---

[12] Robert A. Dahl, Congress and Foreign Policy (New York: Harcourt, Brace and Company, 1950), 258.

secret while the ends are eventually revealed. At the conclusion of a lengthy closed negotiation (or "bargaining conference" as it is referred to in the citation above), the legislature will inevitably be allowed to fully consider the issue.

In the area of defense technology, both the means and the ends most often require a high level of secrecy. In the case of advanced weapons systems, the results of the venture may not be debated with any greater openness than that of the development process. After a program has reached the stage of development at which it might be considered operational, national security grounds for precluding declassification most often continue to exist. In certain situations, secrecy might even become more critical after development has been completed.

Aside from the effects which it has on foreign affairs, sharing defense information with our allies is essential for two main reasons. The first comes from the military's needs for standardization among allied units. Certain weapon systems allow communication interfaces between associated elements. Without such links, cooperation is made very difficult. The second is to contain growing procurement costs by making the process of allied burden-sharing more efficient.[13] U.S. research and

---

[13] John V. Granger, <u>Technology and International Relations</u> (San Francisco: W.H. Freeman and Company, 1979), 75.

development advancements may act to stimulate allied
involvement in similar activities.

Defense Technology and the National Security Threat

Some experts now estimate that a nation's
technological base is in many ways a more indicative measure
of national strength than the traditional measures of
military power.[14] Still others believe that with the Cold
War over, a "technology race" has replaced the traditional
arms race of the past era.[15] In The Rise and Fall of the
Great Powers, Paul Kennedy addressed how the United States
matches the cyclical pattern of overextension and eventual
weakening of powerful nations. He sees the America's
ability to hold on to its technological edge for as long as
possible as a key to preserving U.S. power during the next
century and preventing that power from shifting to other
sources.[16] Certainly such realities represent valid
national security concerns. As a result, the U.S. has

---

[14]   George A. Carver, Jr., "Intelligence in the Age of
Glasnost," Foreign Affairs 69 (1990): 153.

[15]   Paul Kennedy, Preparing for the Twenty-First
Century (New York: Random House, 1993), 127.

[16]   Paul Kennedy, The Rise and Fall of the Great
Powers: Economic Change and Military Conflict from 1500 to
2000 (New York: Random House, 1987) 514.

implemented substantial methods of maintaining the secrecy
of this technology and thereby the resultant competitive
advantage.

This "technology race" is not limited to just
defense. Instead, it includes many other major areas of
scientific development. In 1990, for example, Chairman of
the Senate Select Committee on Intelligence David Boren
noted that: "An increasing share of the espionage directed
against the United States comes from spying by foreign
governments against private American companies aimed at
stealing commercial secrets to gain a national economic
advantage."[17] Nonetheless, defense technology still
represents a consequential segment of that overall race.
From an executive perspective, this direct correlation
between defense technology and overall national power
represents a tremendous need for holding technological
secrets under the most rigid restrictions. The increased
vigor with which U.S. technology is now being pursued by
foreign intelligence agencies greatly magnifies the threat
to national security.

Some commentators believe that technology has acted
as one of the central components in the arms race. The rise
of defense technology over the past fifty years has had a
direct relationship with government secrecy. Since World

---

[17]   George A. Carver, Jr., "Intelligence in the Age of
Glasnost," Foreign Affairs 69 (1990): 154.

War II there has been a tremendous increase in the proportion of national military budgets allocated toward research and development (R&D). During that same period, the quantity of classified defense information has simultaneously risen substantially. High-tech U.S. weapons might characteristically represent significant threats to the U.S.'s own national security if malevolent nations receive the technology necessary to develop them.

Opponents of government secrecy claim that the type of classified defense information which Congress requests is of a benign nature. These critics point out that technical details such as scientific technicalities are included in classified reports to Congress. As a result, the national security danger involved with a release of such information is minimal. Contrary to this statement, many government officials contend that even information which appears trivial to most could prove harmful to U.S. national security. Representative John Kasich (R-OH) argues that,

> When you have a gray program, where there is acknowledgement that such a program exists, then it is all right to talk about the costs...But there are black programs that nobody acknowledges even exist, so it would be a mistake to start putting numbers in the budget that would tip

people off.[18]

Presumably insignificant details, such as the amount
of money spent on an unnamed weapons program, might
represent a valuable piece of data to a foreign intelligence
agency. If minor technicalities are used to uncover the
significance of a program, a foreign government might find a
way to diminish the marginal utility of that program.

Secrecy as a Protector of U.S. Economic Investment

In an age when U.S. defense policy and the economic
state of the union are so closely intertwined, export
controls on nuclear and conventional weapons and related
information are becoming increasingly important. Budgetary
constraints mandate the efficient use of defense resources.
This constitutes another reason why the containment of
classified data is so important. Controlling information on
defense technology allows the United States to maintain a
strategic advantage at a lower cost. In most cases, full
development of a weapon system is not the only maturation
which would make the investment in that program worthwhile.
Maintaining an edge in some field of research allows the

---

[18]   David C. Morrison, "Dancing in the Dark." National
Journal 11 April 1987: 868.

United States to hold a strong bargaining chip in international relations. At the Reykjavik summit, the Strategic Defense Initiative was seen by the Soviets as an important American asset even though that system had not yet been fully developed. During that meeting, the Soviets offered to eliminate all of their offensive strategic arms within ten years if the United States would agree to limit SDI development.[19]

In economic terms, the United States often derives great profits from such technology transfers. In recent years, U.S. defense exports to NATO allies have exceeded imports by ratios as high as eight to one.[20] Today, defense contractors continue to suffer through severe difficulties as a result of the end of the Cold War and the recent economic recession. Overseas markets have been considered by many corporations as a means of preventing further losses. The secrecy of related defense technology must be maintained in order to capitalize on these markets. When such technology is illicitly released before it is marketed abroad, foreign corporations may produce the system without U.S. assistance. If this occurs, American corporations will no longer hold the competitive advantage

---

[19] William J. Broad, Teller's War: The Top Secret Story Behind the Star Wars Deception (New York: Simon & Schuster, 1992), 217.

[20] U.S. Congress, House, Investigations Subcommittee of the Committee on Armed Services, NATO/MOUs, 102nd Cong., 2nd Sess. (Washington, D.C.: G.P.O., 1992), 7.

which they now maintain.

In legal terms, a strong relationship exists between scientific advances in defense technology and the need for secrecy. In the civilian sector, federal patent law contains significant legal restrictions which protect parties who invest resources in research and development. Abraham Lincoln once said, "The patent system... secured to the inventor for a limited time exclusive use of his inventions, and thereby added the fuel of interest to the fire of genius in the discovery and production of new and useful things."[21] In the realm of military research and development, on the other hand, the primary means of protecting this "exclusive use" is through secrecy. Also, understanding the specific details of U.S. weapons systems might allow foreign adversaries to counter them more effectively.

Congress' Inability to Maintain Secrecy
as an Executive Argument for Non-disclosure

Few governments make a greater effort to share classified information with their legislatures than the United States. The efforts that our government takes to insure the distribution of information are certainly based

___

[21]   Guide to American Law, 1984 ed., s.v. "Patents."

upon high principles and provide a model for nations striving to achieve democracy. However, proponents of secrecy maintain that openness may undermine the national security of the United States.

John Jay offered a pessimistic opinion of Congress' ability to withhold secret information from public disclosure while discussing the treaty clause of the Constitution in Federalist number 64.

> There are cases where the most useful intelligence may be obtained if the persons possessing it can be relieved from apprehensions of discovery. Those apprehensions will operate on those persons whether they are actuated by mercenary or friendly motives and there doubtless are many of both descriptions who would rely on the secrecy of the president, but who would not confide in that of the senate and still less in that of a large popular assembly.[22]

When a president cites national security as a reason for denying Congress information, he is often making the implication that the legislature will be unable to retain the secrecy of such material. In recent years, the

---

[22] Alexander Hamilton, James Madison and John Jay, <u>The Federalist</u> (Cambridge, Massachusetts: Harvard University Press, 1961), 422.

level of confidence which the executive branch has in the Congress may have been eroded by what President Bush's National Security Adviser Brent Scowcroft chose to call, "a lack of congressional discipline."[23] From an executive perspective, opening secrets to Congress may require a tremendous expansion of the number of individuals who may access this information. If every member of Congress is allowed to receive a certain classified document, the information is opened to an additional 535 people. Such a high quantity of recipients leaves a very low margin for error. If just one member chooses to reveal this material, that individual would render the measures taken to maintain secrecy 100% ineffective. These numbers are conservative in that they fail to consider the number of congressional staff members who will also be capable of accessing such documents.

The executive branch occasionally finds itself without sufficient means of maintaining the integrity of information once it reaches the Congress. In 1974, Congressman Michael J. Harrington exposed information which had been passed in a classified hearing before the House Armed Services Committee of which he was a member. The records which were made public came from the testimony of Director of Central Intelligence William Colby on covert

---

[23]   Robert L. Pfaltzgraff and Jacquelyn K. Davis, National Security Decisions: The Participants Speak (Lexington, Massachusetts: Lexington Books, 1990), 58.

operations in Chile.[24] As a punishment for his breaking of the rules of the committee and of the House of Representatives, Harrington was prohibited from examining further classified information. Another House Committee avoided a potentially explosive situation by declining to take additional action against him.[25] As it stood, this incident received only minor public and congressional attention. Had stricter penalties been brought against Congressman Harrington, the situation might have precipitated more dramatic exposure. This incident could have provoked yet another major struggle between the Congress and the executive branch over the question of secrecy. Nonetheless, the prudent nature of the action taken left the balance virtually undisturbed.

The relatively light penalty which served as Representative Harrington's punishment is of central interest to opponents of information releases to Congress. While the methods for restricting information are often vague and confusing, the statutes which punish unauthorized disclosure are even less clear. One author described this set of punitive laws as "a veritable mine field of legal

---

[24] Ray S. Cline, Secrets, Spies and Scholars: Blueprint of the Essential CIA (Washington, D.C.: Acropolis Books, 1976), 227.

[25] Howard Frazier, ed., Uncloaking the CIA (New York: The Free Press, 1975), 5.

ambiguities."[26] Although members of the Department of
Defense face severe penalties for releasing classified
defense information, congressional penalties are usually
quite trivial. The lack of an effective means of compelling
Congress to maintain the secrecy of defense information
constitutes a major argument for denying classified
material.

At times, classified materials are shared between
the branches under the trust that the information contained
within will not be released. Supporters of executive
secrecy contend that this trust is often broken. One such
instance occurred in 1975 when a report entitled "The
Performance of the Intelligence Community Before the Arab-
Israeli War of October 1973," was released by the president
to the Select Committee on Intelligence. Part of the
material used in that report was directly quoted from White
House documents. The documents had been provided to
Committee Chairman Otis G. Pike, under the agreement that
certain parts of their contents would not be released. On
September 12, 1975, President Gerald Ford told reporters,

Unfortunately the committee took action that did
not coincide with the agreement that we had with
the committee. And as long as we feel that we had

[26]   Guenter Lewy, "Can Democracy Keep Secrets? Do We
Need an Official Secrets Act?", Policy Review 26 (Fall
1983): 17.

a good faith agreement and it was breached, then I
think that we have proper action in requesting a
return."[27]

Additionally, proponents of secrecy have suggested
that the Congress does not have proper security procedures
available for protecting classified information. While the
Pentagon is a relatively secure environment restricted from
public access, congressional office buildings are open to
visitors. To implement the necessary security precautions
into congressional work environments would require the
implementation of burdensome regulations. These regulations
would create a setting which would be contrary to the
representative nature of Congress.

Another conceivable reason why Congress might
initiate a leak is to increase import earning for the United
States. Exposing the capabilities of an F-16, which might
be manufactured in a Congressman's district, to a foreign
nation could make purchase of that plane more attractive.
However, such disclosures might injure U.S. security if the
exposed technology is unfavorably promoted by the client
nation. Advocates of executive power contend that it is
within the prerogative of the president to conclude how such

---

[27]   U.S., President, Public Papers of the Presidents
of the United States (Washington, D.C.: Office of the
Federal Register, National Archives and Records Service,
1975), Gerald R. Ford, 1975, 1373.

sales should be conducted. The Pentagon's Defense Security Assistance Agency is tasked with regulating international arms trade.

Information leaks may at times lead to a snowball effect. In such a situation, each branch is forced to consecutively disclose further material to prove their integrity to the public. If a member of Congress discloses a classified detail which draws criticism of a particular project, the executive is often forced to make a similar disclosure providing counter information to rectify the situation. In 1987, Senator David Boren provided evidence that the CIA was inappropriately tailoring its reports to support administration policy. Subsequently, CIA Director Robert Gates was compelled to disclose related information to the press, "to correct the public record."[28] By retaining secrecy over classified documents, the executive branch maintains its initiative in the process of releasing information.

Secrecy and the Unity of U.S. Policy

The possible implications of illicit actions taken by members of Congress, such as the ones suggested above,

---

[28] David C. Morrison, "Tilting with Intelligence," National Journal 9 May 1987, 1111.

are considerable. Scholars of information technology, such as Ian Miles and Kevin Robins, define information as an economic resource.[29] With this definition in mind, we may see that an individual representative and the president may find equal value in a certain piece of information. From a decision making perspective, this equality appears necessary. From a foreign policy perspective, a potential for conflict arises. By disseminating information as one sees fit, a member of Congress may both influence and divide the foreign policy of the United States. In the opinion of many officials in the executive branch, restricting the legislative branch from conducting an executive function *should not be considered a nullification of legislative power.*

Proponents of executive power contend that there are sufficient checks on the power of the president which do not invade the unity of the executive branch. One such congressional check on the executive which is relevant to this discussion is the Senate confirmation process. Following presidential appointments, certain potential members of the executive branch are subjected to a vigorous oral examination before a relevant Senate Committee. Before an appointee may assume his office, a majority of the full

---

[29]   Kevin Robins, ed., <u>Understanding Information: Business, Technology and Geography</u> (London: Belhaven Press, 1992), 2.

Senate must vote in favor of the individual. One might find justification in withholding information from Congress in the fact that external checks enumerated in the Constitution provide sufficient oversight of the executive branch.

Inconsistency within the United States government over national security policy matters is often perceived by foreign nations as a sign of weakness or a lack of resolve. A Congress which speaks out against a certain course of action might weaken the apparent authority of a president who is implementing that policy. One method of maintaining the consistency of U.S. foreign policy is through securing the integrity of the executive decision making process. The president often uses secrecy as a main line of defense against congressional infringement of executive unity. It is true that an exclusion of Congress from the activities of foreign relations is not supportive of the need for balanced powers within our framework of government. However, it is evident that duties of Congress and the executive should be reserved to their particular branches when such functions are clearly distinguishable.

When information is released by unofficial sources, two governments are operating in the name of the United States. When the separate branches have diametrically opposed objectives, acting as autonomous governments may greatly compound the intrinsic difficulties of foreign relations. The potential for such a situation seemed to grow in the recent era of divided government. When a release is carefully carried out by the appropriate sources within the executive branch, the result is a unified and controlled policy. Disclosure by an unauthorized source undermines the integrity of this process as well as the unity of the final decision.

Even if Congress is given all the information held by the Department of Defense, decisions concerning research and development would still be murky. The analysis of this information would require a tremendous increase in staff. This would result primarily from the need to interpret the technological complexities inherent in modern weapon systems. Secondly, the volume of information which would be made available would require additional hands to fully assess the material. However, even if this information could be appropriately analyzed, the overall context of the conclusion would be incomplete. Assumptions still would have to be made based on the capabilities of our adversaries. Foreign military capabilities are evaluated by the Central Intelligence Agency and held under strict security constraints.

U.S. intelligence policy itself has been a contentious matter in regards to the debate on secrecy. In certain ways, the debate over the handling of intelligence data is related to the question of defense information. U.S. defense policy must often be judged on the basis of our adversary's power, as was described above. However, the Central Intelligence Agency (CIA) follows a different set of guidelines than those of the Department of Defense (DOD). The Director of Central Intelligence possesses an aegis of legal protection which other members of the executive branch do not hold. The CIA is exempted from a number of the statutes which facilitate congressional oversight and require OMB reports to Congress.[30] In the spectrum of information requirements, the Department of Defense is somewhere between the general openness of the State Department and the nearly unlimited secrecy of the CIA. For this reason, issues related to DOD provide a good point of reference for an extensive discussion of government secrecy.

The issue of the responsibility for ordering military action against a foreign nation is yet another battleground where the issue of secrecy has been fought between the executive and legislative branches. It is obvious that a legislative branch which plays a role in sending troops into combat must have certain information relating to such operations. However, many unique aspects of the war powers issue disconnects this question from our discussion and prevents a thorough consideration of the details in this report.

---

[30]   50 U.S.C., Sec. 403(g) (1970).

A Legal Interpretation in Support of The Executive's Right to Withhold Information

Historically, the national security argument constitutes the primary justification for the executive to withhold classified information. However, certain elements of the Constitution and the law may be cited in support of denying information to Congress. Although a significant vagueness surrounds such legal references, it is necessary to consider how these sources of evidence may be interpreted in favor of the executive.

When one examines the overall system for classifying defense information, it is possible to find a number of reasons supporting these restrictions on classified material within the Constitution. It is ironic that the Constitution is at the same time very specific and very vague about matters of national defense. In very few policy areas does the Constitution specify one role for the Congress and one role for the executive as copiously as it does in this domain. Article I, Section 8 gives Congress the power to declare war while Article II specifies the President as the chief executive. The basis for controversy has come in the process of obtaining a working definition for these terms.[31]

The powers granted to the executive and legislative branches of government overlap in many sections of the U.S. Constitution. The area of national security affairs is one domain in which this has been found to be especially true. The general nature of the Constitution allows for significant confrontation on various matters. This is brought about by the lack of specificity within this document. The realm of secrecy is one area where this flexibility is immediately apparent.

The Constitution makes no specific reference to sharing classified government information between the branches. Some theorists attribute this to the relative insignificance of the issue in the period that the Constitution was drafted. The defense secrets of that era seem relatively benign when compared to the secrets of the latter half of the twentieth century.

Other authors point to additional reasons why the Constitution lacks specificity in this area. Some believe that there were conflicting opinions surrounding the question of secrecy in the early debate of the Constitution. Unresolved arguments might have lead the Founding Fathers to table this issue. Still others believe that the lack of a method for secrecy came as a realization that the issue

---

[31]   George C. Edwards and Wallace Earl Walker, eds., National Security and the U.S. Constitution (Baltimore: Johns Hopkins University Press, 1988), 325.

would take different shapes throughout various points in history.

A lack of specification in the Constitution with respect to secrecy might be interpreted as an authorization for each President and each Congress to find the right balance on its own. The executive might also interpret this lack of specificity to derive support for claiming an exclusive right to information which is generated by its branch. The very nature of defense information means that secrets are originally the property of the executive branch. If the Constitution does not require a release of information, the executive might find no obligation to produce such materials.

In the drafting of the Constitution, very little trust was placed in the virtue of one man or one institution. The systems of checks and balances is based on the theory that men operate best when watched by others. However, the factor of trust overrode any perceived need for oversight in many areas of national security throughout early American history. This might account for yet another reason why the question of secrecy received very little question until recent times. The appearance of executive corruption, as was seen in such events as the Pentagon Papers and Watergate, lead critics to reevaluate the oversight structure. Members of Congress began to doubt whether confidence in the opposite branch of government was enough of a check on its power. As a result, Congress execution of its oversight responsibility switched from "benign neglect" to "zealous overreaching".[32] However, it is important to note that there is a significant precedent of trust within American history. For many years this very trust acted as the basis for neglecting to check the balance of secrecy.

A fine example of the use of trust as a viable alternative to an active check on executive power may be found in the example below. In the confirmation hearings of former CIA director Richard Helms in February of 1973, Senator Gale McGee commended Mr. Helms for his performance at the CIA. Discussing his previous record, he stated,

> I would join my voice with those who have
> applauded your leadership where you have been. I
> think that has been refreshing and it has enhanced
> the credibility of the CIA and its role...I guess
> I would have to confess without knowing all the
> details, that I would sleep better if you were
> still there, but that is no reflection of your

---

[32] David Everett Colton, "Speaking Truth to Power: Intelligence Oversight in an Imperfect World," <u>University of Pennsylvania Law Review</u> 137 (1988): 582.

successor.[33]

An intelligence officer from the CIA said that, "men like Richard Helms are the cream of the crop in our society. If we can't trust them to do what's right, who can we trust."[34] Some of the verbiage found in the confirmation hearing is typical, where witnesses are commended for prior service to the nation. However, the element of leadership may it times shift the secrecy balance in favor of the executive branch.

Another general citation which presidents have invoked is the controversial proclamation of executive privilege. Executive privilege has been defined as, "the President's claim of constitutional authority to withhold information to the Congress."[35] The use of the term "executive privilege" did not come about until 1953 when it was used in the petitioners brief for Certiorari in United

---

[33]   U.S. Congress. Senate. Committee on Foreign Relations. Nomination of Richard Helms to be Ambassador to Iran and CIA International and Domestic Activities. 93rd Cong., 1st Sess. (Washington, D.C.: G.P.O., 1974), 6.

[34]   Loch K. Johnson, A Season of Inquiry: The Senate Intelligence Investigation (Lexington: University of Kentucky Press, 1985), 7-8.

[35]   Raoul Berger, Executive Privilege: A Constitutional Myth (Cambridge, Massachusetts: Harvard University Press, 1974), 1.

States v. Reynolds.[36]   Since then, its very existence has been a point of heated controversy.   As a general basis for information withholding it has received passionate criticism from such legal scholars as Raoul Berger, Robert Kramer and Herman Marcuse.   Codified laws such as the Classified Information Procedures Act of 1980 furnish a more concrete basis for the assertion of executive power.   The power to classify information belongs solely to the executive under current law.   Presidential efforts to exercise and maintain exclusive rights over such information have not originated until quite recently.

The War Power Debate as a Legal Standard of Reference

Within the Constitution, the debates over war powers and secrecy parallel one another in many ways.   As was stated above, examining these two issues together from a policy perspective may become confusing. Nonetheless, the legal interpretations of these two points of contention are quite comparable.   Many sections of the Constitution which are cited in discussions of war powers are equally relevant to our evaluation of secrecy.   Examining these two issues side by side will attribute to the problems involved in legal interpretations of the secrecy balance.

---

[36]   Paul A. Fruend, "The Supreme Court, 1973 Term: Foreword: On Presidential Privilege."(Harvard Law Review 88 (1974)) 18.

Constitutional instructions concerning the war powers are quite substantial, although not prolific. Nonetheless, many of the recent armed conflicts which have been initiated by the executive were denounced as infringements of the power allocated to Congress by the Constitution. On the other hand, hardly a word is dedicated to the question of secrecy. With this in mind, it is possible to comprehend the troubles which will be encountered when secrecy is approached from a legal perspective. The intensity of debate surrounding the War Powers Resolution is indicative of the controversy which one encounters when secrecy becomes the focus of study. Such complexities might lead one to believe that there is no definite answer to this question of secrecy. While this may not be all together true, it adds credibility to the assertion that the Constitution might not be the most potent weapon in either the executive's or the legislature's arsenal.

CONGRESSIONAL JUSTIFICATIONS FOR INFORMATION DISCLOSURE
Defense Information in
Congressional Decision Making

In the first section, the importance of executive secrecy was weighed in terms of its effects on national security. In order to place our results into a balance with congressional requirements, Congress' need for information must be established. The first step in the process of considering the question of secrecy from a legislative perspective is to define what information is needed by the Congress. Once we have made this specification, we may consider how this additional knowledge affects the decision making process.

The executive may broadly authorize extensive secrecy over a wide range of information under the comprehensive term "national security". When we shift our view to a congressional perspective, we must attempt to create a more exact definition of the term information. Congress' needs for information are extremely specific and localized in comparison to the enormous collection of data held by the Department of Defense.

Despite specific congressional needs, lawmakers have historically been unable to find an equally specific legal definition for the information which it requires. In addition, Congress has found even greater difficulty in drafting a definition that is acceptable to the executive branch. Nonetheless, it is possible to develop general boundaries which do not excessively infringe on the essential powers of either branch. As a result, it is not our goal to define the term information. Instead, we seek only to sufficiently narrow it.

Some critics of government secrecy, including
Morton Halperin and Daniel Hoffman, have concluded that the
only defense information which should be classified is that
which pertains to technicalities of weapon systems, plans
for military operations, details of diplomatic negotiations
and intelligence procedures.[37] According to this theory,
all other information is outside the "legitimate boundaries"
of national security information and should therefore be
released to Congress. For the purposes of this report, we
may adopt the Halperin and Hoffman model as an acceptable
means of confining the boundaries of this general term.[38]

Creating a precise definition of what information
will be released to Congress is of limited importance for
additional reasons. Each member of Congress has his or her
own requirements for information. One intellectual member
might spend numerous hours each evening reviewing scholarly
journals. To another member, the information available in

---

[37] A. DeVolpi and others, <u>Born Secret: The H-Bomb,
The Progressive Case and National Security</u> (New York:
Pergamon Press, 1981), 132.

[38] Halperin, Hoffman and others have called for a
definition of defense information which requires more
specific guidelines. Proponents of secrecy would claim that
such action would excessively infringe upon the rights of
the executive. The thesis of this report maintains that the
legal guidelines for information disclosure play only a
minor role in the overall secrecy balance. Whereas the
balance frequently shifts in favor of one branch or the
other, creating a rigid definition for this term is both
unnecessary and inaccurate. The definition provided
reflects the circumstances of an average location of the
secrecy balance.

such publications might be irrelevant. Similarly, we may
immediately assume that any resultant balance of secrecy
will leave certain members with too much information, while
others are found with not enough. The optimal situation
from an executive perspective is achieved when the number of
members who have enough information exceeds the number with
inadequate information by one.

Before one may go on to place the concept of
information into the context of congressional decision-
making, it is necessary to make a distinction between
information and data. Data might be defined as, "the raw
facts and figures from which information is created."
Information, by comparison, "consists of facts and data that
have been organized into conceptual frameworks."[39] In
order to illustrate this difference, we may consider an
example from World War II. Before the Japanese attack on
Pearl Harbor, the United States had deciphered many of
Japan's secret cryptographic codes. Although the United
States held a great deal of data before the attack, it
remained unintelligible. In effect, the United States
lacked complete information and therefore an understanding
of how the accumulation of details fit together. Without a
certain level of understanding of the collected data, the
raw materials obtained by the U.S. were proven to be

---

[39]   Stephen E. Frantzich. Computers in Congress: The
Politics of Information. Beverly Hills: Sage Publications,
1982.

worthless.[40]

Although a member of Congress may receive
classified data, it will be rendered useless if the member
has no means of analyzing it. Quite often, the professional
expertise held by members of Congress lies outside the realm
of technical experience. For this reason, allowing Congress
to review classified information often requires subsequent
disclosure to staff members who have an expertise in this
field.

In every systematic method of thought, decision
makers must analyze information. Some behavioral scientists
group this element of the decision making process under the
title, "Generating alternative choices."[41] While the
definition of this step varies from one theory to another,
it is almost universally accepted that comprehensive
information relating to the relevant issue facilitates the
effective resolution of a problem. Therefore, whereas
Congress is a decision making body, its overall
effectiveness will be directly proportional to the
thoroughness of the information it receives.

At times, a level of uncertainty exists within the
decision making process due to a lack of information

---

[40] William H. Robinson and Clay H. Wellborn, eds.,
Knowledge, Power and the Congress (Washington, D.C.:
Congressional Quarterly, 1991), 174.

[41] John D. Mullen and Byron M. Roth, Decision Making:
It's Logic and Practice (Savage, Maryland: Rowman and
Littlefield Publishers, 1991), 3.

concerning the question at hand. This condition often continues throughout the numerous stages of the legislative procedure. Such uncertainty is especially relevant when national defense issues are addressed due to the security restrictions surrounding much of the related information. In such cases, the consequences of decisions do not become apparent until either the information is released or the final outcome of the process is realized.[42] Applying this assertion to congressional decision making regarding classified national defense issues, one begins to realize the problems involved with maintaining strict secrecy restrictions. The final outcome of the overall procedure is quite often not achieved until many years have passed. In the meantime, Congress is often tasked with making numerous further decisions along the way.

There are a number of negative implications of awaiting the final outcome of the decision making process while defense information is continuously withheld. These effects may be observed by conducting a preliminary analysis of the Strategic Defense Initiative. In the FY1984 defense appropriation and authorization bills, Congress was tasked with making a decision on SDI without having complete information regarding the program. Members were also faced with similar dilemmas during the following years. In 1988,

---

[42]   C. J. McKenna, The Economics of Uncertainty (New York: Oxford University Press, 1986), 8.

for example, the outcome of the decision making process undertaken in 1984 was still unknown. During that same year, however, members of Congress were faced with making yet another decision on SDI. As Congress now addresses the FY1994 authorization bill, part of the program which they approved ten years ago remains to be uncovered. Thus, the congressional decision making process defense is faced with a multiplier effect when classified information is withheld over an extended period. Five million dollars appropriated one year might properly be visualized as such. Nonetheless, this appropriation also represents a limited fraction of a much larger total, the cumulative accretion of SDI appropriations.

The theoretical concepts of decision making continue to be advanced to this day in such fields as modern economic choice theory.[43] The choice theory for example provides a logical method for rational decision making in everyday situations. A good choice, according to this model, is one which "considers alternatives in terms of their outcomes."[44] For some time, writings on the specific elements of rational decision making were mainly considered by economists, behavioral scientists and other scholars. However, some lawmakers and government officials have

---

[43]   David M. Levy, The Economic Ideas of Ordinary People. (New York: Routledge, 1992), 109.

[44]   James G. March, Decisions and Organizations (New York: Basil Blackwell, 1988), 2.

recently begun to use theories regarding the economics of uncertainty to systematically analyze certain public policy issues. To date, these methods have only been used to manage such problems as safety and health.[45] In such policy areas, the information needed to draw a conclusion is more than just concealed, it simply does not exist.

While these concepts have gained some acceptance, they remain highly theoretical. Examination of these theories are relevant to the question of secrecy in regards to the deficiencies they bring with them. Even the inventors of these theories would concede that they provide results which are inferior to the conclusions acquired through reasoned decision making based on complete data. Although extensive research has been conducted by political economists, psychologists and other experts in attempts to overcome these obstacles, there is simply no substitute to thorough details which are applicable to a question at hand.

Researchers across the full spectrum of disciplines concede that theories on decision making are rather speculative. Some go so far as to concede that uncertainties in the processes of rational decision making render them as, "Nothing but a model," which man rarely follows anyway.[46] However, few would disagree with the

---

[45] Jack Hirshleifer, Time, Uncertainty and Information (New York: Basil Blackwell, 1989), 153.

[46] Israel M. Kirzner, Discovery, Capitalism, and Distributive Justice (New York: Basil Blackwell, 1989), 38.

principle "that economic agents prefer to have better information if they can acquire it."[47] In some policy areas, information regarding a problem does not exist. By comparison, information concerning defense technology often does exist. However, it is concealed from those who make decisions on it for the reason of national security.

Officials of the executive branch argue that if certain defense secrets fall into the hands of our adversaries, we will lose the competitive advantage which the product might have brought to our defense establishment. It is apparent that both the executive's need for confidentiality and the Congress' requirements for information are essential for an effective and efficient military. Our analysis will demonstrate how this balance may not be struck through rational analysis. Instead, it must follow a dynamic interaction between the executive and legislative branches of government.

Congressional Means of Obtaining Information

While each member of Congress has an equal vote on the floor, they each do not hold equivalent means for requesting information. Before the Cuban Missile Crisis

---

[47] Louis Phlips, The Economics of Imperfect Information (New York: Cambridge University Press, 1988), 12.

became public, seventeen congressional leaders met with President Kennedy for a briefing. What the other sixteen members did not know, however, was that one of their peers, Senator Richard Russell, had already been informed of the developments. Prior to this meeting, Russell had asked for a briefing on Cuba. Due to his prominent status in Congress, the President decided that it was important that he be given a complete representation of the situation. As a result, the predicament was secretly revealed to the Senator.[48] This case displays more than a double standard; it shows a "layered" approach to information release. On the top layer was Senator Russell, who used his lofty position to gain immediate access. Later, sixteen additional members of the leadership were notified. Finally, Congress would be notified in its entirety.

The primary means by which Congress may require a member of the executive to provide information is by calling that individual to testify before a congressional committee. Title two of the United States Code strictly requires the attendance of every person who is summoned as a witness to appear before a given committee. According to this act, failure to appear or refusal, "To answer any question pertinent to the question under inquiry," may result in

---

[48] Michael R. Beschloss, The Crisis Years: Kennedy and Kruschev, 1960-1963 (New York: Harper Collins Publishers, 1991), 480.

criminal action against the witness. The witness may be brought before a grand jury and found guilty of a misdemeanor. This offense carries a sentence of up to twelve months imprisonment. The statute provides no exemptions for matters regarding national security information.[49]

Both houses of Congress may use their subpoena power to require the disclosure of documents and to mandate the attendance of a witness before a committee. The Congress has the authority to hold a witness in contempt if he or she refuses to answer a pertinent question in a committee hearing. According to title two of the U.S. Code, such an action may result in a fine of up to $1,000 and a year imprisonment.[50] Although Congress officially must have a legislative purpose for its request for information, such a purpose need not be specified in advance. In most cases, the subject of the hearing itself will point toward the purpose of the inquiry.[51]

Since 1798, Congressional committees have had the option of administering oaths to witnesses. However, most testimony received before Congress is provided by

---

[49]   2 U.S.C., Sec. 192 (1938).

[50]   U.S. Congress. Joint Committee on Congressional Operations. Leading Cases on Congressional Investigatory Power. 94th Cong., 2d Sess. (Washington, D.C.: G.P.O., 1976), 2.

[51]   U.S. Congress. Joint Committee on Congressional Operations. Leading Cases on Congressional Investigatory Power. 94th Cong., 2d Sess. (Washington, D.C.: G.P.O., 1976), 7.

individuals who have not been sworn in. The difference
between the two scenarios is that sworn witnesses who make
false statements may be convicted of perjury. In general,
it is much more difficult to convict an unsworn witness.
Additionally, penalties for offenses not made under oath are
mild by comparison.[52] In their codified forms, the
procedures for prosecution seem uncomplicated while the
penalties appear significant. In reality, the statutes are
seldom used whereas guilt is hard to establish. Sentences
which have been awarded have fallen far short of those which
are cited in the code. In most cases the punishment is
merely a fine.

Classified information is not handled by all
members of Congress on a regular basis. Throughout all
elements of society, we may find that, "The time and effort
necessary to acquire knowledge are minimized through
specialization."[53] Congress' method of specialization is
the committee system. Although the House and Senate Armed
Services Committees frequently hold hearings in closed
session, they are not the only committees which have a need
for classified information. The Foreign Affairs, Judiciary,
and Appropriations Committees often need secret information

---

[52]   James Hamilton, The Power to Probe: A Study of
Congressional Investigations (New York: Random House, 1976),
75.

[53]   Thomas Sowell, Knowledge and Decisions (New York:
Basic Books, 1980), 7.

for consideration of matters under their jurisdiction. For example, the Subcommittee on Arms Control, International Security and Science of the House Foreign Affairs Committee held at least five hearings during the One Hundred Second Congress concerning issues regarding conventional arms transfer policy. In order for committees to judge whether authorizations of sales such as the F-15 Aircraft to Saudi Arabia are in the best interest of national security, a certain amount of information regarding the aircraft is necessary.

Congressional Rebuttal to
the National Security Argument

As was stated before, arguments of the executive for withholding information from Congress have been based on the threat which these releases would pose to U.S. national security. Members of Congress often argue that they are able to maintain the secrecy of classified material as well as, if not better than, the executive branch.

Proponents of executive power have occasionally argued that Congress may legally avoid the obligation of preserving the secrecy of information. Some have offered that Congress can find reprieve in the debate clause of Section I of the Constitution. This clause states that, "for any Speech or Debate in either House, they [Senators and Representatives] shall not be questioned in any other Place."[54] A 1989 Congressional Research Service Report for Congress addressed the legal issues associated with the release of classified information by members of Congress. This report thoroughly examined whether the debate clause could be used as a defense from criminal prosecution. The article concludes that the clause does in most cases provide immunity from prosecution under criminal law. However, it does not, "foreclose the possible application of internal controls and sanctions which could be applied by its own members for conduct which that legislative body deemed inappropriate."[55]

If unauthorized disclosure of classified information is made by a member of Congress, that member may not find legal reprieve by claiming the material is not harmful to national security. In such a case, the government is not required to prove the injury which the release would cause. By law, leaks of confidential material will be, "Presumed to cause at least identifiable damage to national security."[56] This leaves little room for members

---

[54]   Constitution, art. I, sec. 6, cl. 1.

[55]   U.S. Library of Congress, Congressional Research Service, Legal Issues Related to the Possible Release of Classified Information by Senators, Representatives or Members of Their Staffs, by Elizabeth B. Bazan, May 22, 1989, CRS Report 89-322A, 13.

[56]   A. DeVolpi and others, Born Secret: The H-Bomb, The Progressive Case and National Security, (New York: Pergamon Press, 1981), 139.

of Congress to avoid the constraints of the law.

Legal and Constitutional Limitations of The
Executive's Exclusive Right to Classified Information

After a thorough consideration of the basis of arguments for and against secrecy, the reasons most often cited come from two specific sources. Support for significant control over information by the executive comes from needs for operational efficiency in foreign and national security affairs. By comparison, arguments for increased Congressional power mainly stem from the Constitution.

According to the Constitution, the Congress has the power to, "Provide for the common Defense and general Welfare of the United States," and, "Provide for calling forth the militia."[57] In addition, the Congress may, "Declare War."[58] and, "Make rules for the Government and Regulation of the land and naval Forces."[59]

The most powerful, and to some experts the only, citation from the Constitution which may be used as a justification for information disclosure is the power of the

---

[57]   Constitution, art. I, sec. 8, cl. 1.

[58]   Constitution, art. I, sec. 8, cl. 11.

[59]   Constitution, art. I, sec. 8, cl. 14.

purse.[60] According to Article I, Section 9 of the
Constitution, "No money shall be drawn from the Treasury,
but in Consequence of Appropriations made by Law."[61] When
Congress allows the executive to leave large gaps in the
budget for secret projects which are not reviewed before an
appropriate committee, it does more than fail to use its
appropriations power. In effect, it delegates that power to
the executive branch.

Another citation from the Constitution which
might be used in support of the distribution of classified
information to Congress is the commerce clause. Although
this segment of the Constitution has been heavily litigated,
little action has been seen in the courts where it is placed
in a national security context. Article I, Section 8
provides Congress the power, "To regulate Commerce with
foreign Nations."[62] As was explained earlier, many defense
contractors have increased their reliance on overseas sales
since the end of the Cold War. It was suggested that the
secrecy of defense technology must be strictly maintained so
that U.S. firms might maintain a competitive advantage in
this markets. The commerce clause might fortify the
argument that Congress should be granted access to related

---

[60] David Everett Colton, "Speaking Truth to Power:
Intelligence Oversight in an Imperfect World," University of
Pennsylvania Law Review 137 (1988): 589.

[61] Constitution, art. I, sect. 9, cl. 7.

[62] Constitution, art. I, sec. 8, cl. 3.

information so that it might properly execute its oversight function.

The final clause of Article I, Section 8 gives Congress the power, "To make all laws necessary and proper for carrying into Execution...all other powers vested in the Government of the United States."[63] This broad authorization is often cited by those who favor an increase in congressional power. The clause, in some regards, might form the backbone for congressional arguments in battles between the Congress and the President over foreign affairs. The phrase "necessary and proper" is extremely vague and allows for significant claims to power. In this way it is similar to the president's sometimes equivocal use of the term national security as an excuse for withholding information. Critics of the overexpansion of congressional power might claim that the clause has allowed the Congress to overextend its legislative power. Despite its lack of specificity, the clause is cited in Section 2 of Public Law 93-148, the now famous War Powers Act,[64] as the primary

---

[63]   Constitution, art. I, sec. 8, cl. 17.

[64]   This controversial resolution was passed over the veto of President Nixon on Nov. 7, 1973 in the effort to assure that both the executive and the Congress share in the decision to involve U.S. forces in combat. According to this statute, the president has 90 days to receive the approval of the Congress when he chooses to engage forces in hostilities against an enemy.

Constitutional justification for the resolution.[65]

While the restrictions on the access to government information are not clearly specified, the Constitution and the early debate surrounding it were not devoid of the mention of secrecy. Article I, Section 5 states that, "Each House shall keep a Journal of its Proceedings, and from time to time publish the same, excepting such Parts as may in their Judgement require Secrecy."[66] This clause might hint that information introduced into a large body such as the U.S. House of Representatives might remain secret if appropriately classified. Additionally, it might undermine some of the arguments that national security information should be released to the general public.

Basing the test for the need to maintain secrecy on "Judgement" provides Congress substantial liberty to withhold information as it sees fit. The fact that there is no parallel clause in support of the executive's right to maintain secrets adds to the furtive and abstract nature of this executive power.

The concept of separation of powers within the Constitution is based on the premise of suspicion. In other words, the Constitution encourages the Congress and the

---

[65] Congress, House, Committee on Foreign Affairs, The War Powers Resolution: A Special Study of the Committee on Foreign Affairs, Committee Print, 97th Cong., 2d Sess., 1982, p. 287.

[66] Constitution, Art. I, Sec. 5, cl. 3.

President to suspect the intentions and jurisdiction of each other. The antithesis of suspicion is the principle of confidence. Per this tenet, one government body allows another to behave in an acceptable manner. Quite often, American political scientists look to the English relationship between the Cabinet and the House of Commons as a prime example for this sort of government. However, American political tradition provides numerous areas where this concept might be present in a de facto sense. One example of this is when Congress fails to consider the classified defense information to which it has access.[67] However, Congress does have the power to mobilize its suspicion of the executive in the oversight process.

Congress requires classified information in order to fulfill its legislative duty of oversight. Earlier, it was mentioned that the executive branch holds a keen interest in keeping members of Congress accountable for the classified information which it is granted. Similarly, Congress seeks oversight of the secrets held by the executive in order to hold that branch accountable. It is conceivable that a President who works under a shadow of confidentiality might have to answer to neither the Congress nor the public.

For years, ineffective oversight on behalf of

---

[67]   Robert A. Dahl, Congress and Foreign Policy (New York: Harcourt, Brace and Company, 1950), 206.

Congress was not due to a lack of information. Instead, Congress fell short in that it did not desire additional information and was even indifferent to information it was given. For most members of Congress, the political payoff for such oversight activities was minimal. The difficult task of probing the immense federal bureaucracy represented the expenditure of a tremendous amount of time. Most members came to believe that this time might be better spent on matters which were more relevant to their constituencies. In June 1975, Senator Frank Church said, "I remember when I first came to the Senate, some of these senior senators who did have this so-called watchdog committee were known to say in effect, 'We don't watch the dog. We don't know what's going on, and furthermore, we don't want to know.'"[68] Certainly such an approach to oversight does not fit into the Constitutional model of checks and balances.

One legislative power which is not often cited as a reason for information disclosure to Congress is the Senate's power to advise and consent on the matter of treaties.[69] It has been stated that imperfect or incomplete information is the root of conflict in

---

[68] Loch K. Johnson, A Season of Inquiry: The Senate Intelligence Investigation (Lexington: University of Kentucky Press, 1985), 6.

[69] Constitution, art. 2, sec. 2, cl. 2.

international relations.[70]   Whereas Congress plays a role
in foreign activities as a result of its treaty power,
unrooting this source of conflict is advantageous to all
parties involved.   Pursuant to this power, the Secretary of
State is required by law to deliver, "the text of any
international agreement."   Under title one of the United
States Code, the executive branch is under no obligation to
provide details of the negotiation process.[71]

Some provisions in various international arms
reduction agreements touch on matters that might require an
advanced understanding of a weapons system in question.   For
example, a clause in a treaty might state that the United
States agrees to eliminate twenty-five of U.S. Trident
missiles in exchange for the elimination of fifty russian
SS-25 missiles.   Knowing the capabilities of this system is
essential to drawing a proper conclusion on the agreement.
Other information which one might use to draw his conclusion
is the state of U.S. research and development on other
defense projects.

---

[70]   Arthur A. Stein, Why Nations Cooperate:
Circumstances and Choice in International Relations (Ithaca,
New York: Cornell University Press, 1990), 13.

[71]   1 U.S.C., Sec. 112(b) (1978).

POLITICAL ANALYSIS OF SECRECY
Secrecy as a Political Device

When considered as remote entities, the popular reasons for shifting the secrecy balance simply do not have a major effect on the issue. The national security threat posed by releasing classified information to Congress is infinitesimal. The legal arguments used by the Congress to force the surrender of secret documents carry no repercussions for non-compliance. With these cursory explanations set aside, we must look for a more substantive reason why the secrecy balance changes.

Our search for the significant forces which act on the secrecy balance will be handled in two stages. The first stage will consist of an historical review of the secrecy balance. This phase of analysis will be followed by a discussion of the means by which secrecy is often exploited. The second stage of this investigation will consist of a case study of the Strategic Defense Initiative. This case study will demonstrate nine main elements of the intragovernmental battle over SDI that show the political nature of this struggle.

There are many intrinsic dangers in indiscriminately concluding that political power is the predominant force in the battle over secrecy. Quite often,

observers of government impulsively label the systematic
resolution of public policy issues as commonplace examples
of pure politics, implying that the solution lacks reasoned
judgement. A clear danger exists in impetuously presuming
such conclusions. Instead, we will attempt to conduct a
more comprehensive examination of the political aspects of
information requests and releases. This shall provide a
more reasoned understanding to this issue.

Historical Evolution of the Secrecy Balance

The legal references considered in previous
sections have occasionally been proposed as means of
securing the position of secrecy at a particular equilibrium
point. However, secrecy is a concept which may not be
easily fixed at some given position. Countless attempts at
creating an immutable position for the balance of secrecy
have attained minimal success. The most monumental efforts
have resulted in little more than shifting the balance in
favor of either the executive or the legislative branch.
Throughout American history, the balance of secrecy has
moved from one position to another as a result of various
pressures from specific sources. When we examine the
history of secrecy, we may identify the forces which act on
this balance and the relevant impact which these forces

have.

Perhaps the first instance in American history when Congress and the president came into conflict over the issue of secrecy came in 1792. On this occasion, George Washington and his cabinet recognized the potential for conflict regarding secrecy. In March 1792, the House of Representatives requested information regarding the failure of a military expedition lead by General Arthur St. Clair. During the first month of this expedition, the company suffered heavy desertions and inclement weather. On November 3, the party traveled late into the evening and retired without taking the necessary security precautions. That night, an Indian band attacked and took the lives of 600 officers and soldiers.[72] Washington decided that since this was the first time the Congress requested executive papers, the matter should receive thorough consideration so as not to set a spurious precedent.[73] After thorough debate amongst the cabinet, they resolved:

First, that the House was an inquest, and

---

[72] U.S. Congress. House. Subcommittee of the Committee on Government Operations. _Availability of Information to Congress_. 95th Cong., 1st Sess. H.R. Res. 4938, 5983, 6438. (Washington: GPO, 1973), 265.

[73] U.S. Congress. Senate. Subcommittee on Constitutional Rights of the Committee on the Judiciary. _The Power of the President to Withhold Information from the Congress: Memorandums of the Attorney General_. 85th Cong., 2nd Sess. (Washington: G.P.O., 1958), 4.

therefore might institute inquiries. Second, that it might call for papers generally. Third, that the Executive ought to communicate such papers as the public good would permit, and ought to refuse those, the disclosure of which would injure the public: consequently were to exercise a discretion. Fourth, that neither the committee nor House had a right to call on the Head of a Department, who and whose papers were under the President alone; but that the committee should instruct their chairman to move the house to address the President.[74]

Thus from the very outset of the debate on secrecy, it was apparent that the balance would be loosely constrained by broad restrictions. Saying that information would be passed, "As the public good permits," left the executive branch tremendous latitude to act with its discretion on such matters. At the time when this statement was made, the interpretation received little attention. As a result, the original battle over secrecy left tremendous power in the hands of the executive.

Although the occurrences of 1792 passed without major incident, the newly formed nation was soon faced with

---

[74] Thomas Jefferson, The Writings of Thomas Jefferson, Vol. I (Washington, D.C.: The Thomas Jefferson Memorial Association, 1904), 304.

its first highly contentious battle over secrecy. In 1795,
Chief Justice John Jay returned from London with a treaty
which quickly became extremely unpopular. Enraged at the
numerous benefits which the treaty designated for the
Federalists, members of the House of Representatives called
for a release of all the documents and correspondence
surrounding the treaty.

Washington agreed to release the documents to the
Senate, noting that such information was necessary for that
body to properly carry forth its constitutional role of
approving treaties. However, he refused to pass the same
information to the House, on the grounds that the
Constitution had afforded that body no role in the
negotiation of treaties. The house, enraged by the refusal,
threatened to withhold funds necessary for the
implementation of the treaty.[75] Debate of the matter
reached such a level of intensity that many feared it would
lead to the dissolution of the Union.[76] In order to avoid
such a fate, the house finally appropriated the needed
funds.

One of the first sets of regulations concerning
secrecy which was enacted into laws was the Espionage Act of

---

[75] Wilfred Ellsworth Binkley, President and Congress
(New York: Alfred A. Knopf, 1947), 43-44.

[76] Claude G. Bowers, Jefferson and Hamilton: The
Struggle for Democracy in America (Cambridge, Massachusetts:
The Riverside Press, 1925), 398.

1917. This statute made it unlawful to gather, transmit or
lose classified defense information. That act set a maximum
penalty of ten years imprisonment for such an offense.[77]
Up until the second World War, the lack of high technology
weapons systems made most defense secrets of little
relevance to individuals outside of the military. This
statute was directed mainly toward operational information.

The emergence of atomic energy brought with it a
series of new laws that prohibited the unlawful disclosure
of relevant data. This segment of secrecy law originated
with the Atomic Energy Act of 1946. Although that act has
been amended significantly since, it continues to provide a
foundation for arguments against disclosure to this day.
These efforts to prevent the accidental exposure of
government secrets came in the wake of increased foreign
efforts to obtain such information. At the time of its
passage, little attention was paid towards how these
restrictions would affect Congress itself. Once again,
tremendous initiative was placed in the hands of the
executive branch.

One of the first major shifts of the secrecy
balance in favor of the Congress came less than ten years
after passage of the Atomic Energy Act. Some observers
recognize 1955 as the milestone year in which Congress

---

[77]   18 U.S.C., Sec. 793(f) (1917).

reversed the momentum of the secrecy balance.[78] That June, Congress created the Subcommittee on Government Information and named Representative John E. Moss (D-CA) as its first chairman. The Subcommittee conducted extensive oversight and initiated significant legislation which improved information policies. In 1963, this Subcommittee was combined with another to form the Subcommittee on Foreign Operations and Government Information.[79]

There is a lack of statistics on the frequency of conflicts between the branches concerning information. This is due in large part to the fact that many additional information denials undoubtedly occur in closed session without the creation of public debate. It has been estimated, however, that between 1964 and 1973 there were 283 instances when the executive branch refused to meet Congress' information requests.[80] This era might be interpreted as one in which the balance of secrecy rested in favor of the executive.

---

[78] U.S. Congress, Senate, Subcommittee on Constitutional Rights of the Committee on the Judiciary, The Power of the President to Withhold Information from the Congress: Memorandums of the Attorney General, 85th Cong., 2nd Sess. (Washington: G.P.O., 1958), 2.

[79] Thomas M. Franck and Edward Weisband, eds., Secrecy and Foreign Policy (New York: Oxford University Press, 1974), 77.

[80] Paul C. Rosenthal and Robert S. Grossman, "Congressional Access to Confidential Information Collected by Federal Agencies," Harvard Journal on Legislation 15 (1977): 117.

Quite often, public policy decisions are made as responses to negative experiences in American history. In the early 1970's, the increase in the call for less secrecy in government came in large part to intelligence agency abuses. While only some of the allegations made against the CIA in this era turned out to be true, a negative perception remained.[81] This negative public opinion aided the Congress in stripping part of the executive's secrecy power.

The case of the United States v. Nixon was one of the rare occasions in which the judicial branch has chosen to rule on an issue of secrecy. It must be noted that this case did not attempt to find an exact position for the balance between the needs of presidential secrecy and congressional information. Instead, it merely constrained the range in which this balance could swing. In this case, the balance shifted away from the president due to the lack of a national security threat.

Earlier, national security was described as a term which may include an extremely wide realm. In the Nixon case, the court ruled that the executive had attempted to define a national security threat outside of this expansive realm. In later cases which came as an aftermath of Watergate, the court would again reaffirm its position that secrecy is a political question. In these decisions, it was

---

[81] David Everett Colton, "Speaking Truth to Power: Intelligence Oversight in an Imperfect World," University of Pennsylvania Law Review 137 (1988): 572.

stated that the position of the secrecy balance was a battle over turf between the executive and the Congress. The judicial branch most often refuses to rule on such disputes.

The CIA has often been the source of outrage over the negative effects of secrecy. The Senate Select Committee to Study Governmental Operations with Respect to Intelligence conducted a thorough investigation of the CIA in 1974 and 1975 under the chairmanship of Senator Frank Church. The Committee found numerous adverse practices occurring at the Agency including assassination attempts on foreign leaders and the opening of American mail.[82] This continued to shift the balance of secrecy in favor of the Congress.

On November 14, 1975, the House Select Intelligence Committee voted 10-2 to hold Secretary of State Kissinger in contempt of Congress. The decision came in the wake of Kissinger's refusal to release eight documents regarding covert intelligence operations which were subpoenaed by the committee on November 5.[83] While Kissinger called the charges "frivolous", they represented a significant embarrassment to the administration both at home and

---

[82] Joseph E. Persico, Casey: From the OSS to the CIA (New York: Penguin Books, 1990), 213.

[83] "Pike Committee: Kissinger Contempt Citation," Congressional Quarterly Weekly Report 33 (1975): 2506.

abroad.[84] In a November 19 letter to Chairman Otis G. Pike, President Ford cited executive privilege and argued that the administration had already given his committee "unprecedented access to Executive Branch documents and information."[85] On December 11, the committee withdrew the charges and thereby "spared what would have been a catastrophic confrontation with the Congress."[86]

In the wake of Watergate, President Ford made significant attempts to share information with Congress, realizing that he would become culpable for previous scandals only if it appeared that he was covering them up.[87] On this occasion, the President himself aided in the shift of the secrecy continuum towards greater openness. Some feel that these and other consequences of the Watergate experience caused the balance of secrecy to excessively shift away from the executive branch. As one British observer stated, "In the aftermath of Watergate, the American people seemed to have gone overboard in their

---

[84] Judy Gardner, "House to Vote: Pike Pushes Kissinger Contempt Citations," Congressional Quarterly Weekly Report 33 (1975): 2572.

[85] "Ford Message to Rep. Pike on Contempt Issue." Congressional Quarterly Weekly Report, 29 November 1975, 2589.

[86] Gerald R. Ford, A Time to Heal: The Autobiography of Gerald R. Ford (New York: Harper & Row Publishers, 1979), 357.

[87] Ron Nessen, It Sure Looks Different from the Inside (New York: Simon and Schuster, 1978), 60.

pursuit of U.S. classified documents."[88]

During his two terms in office, President Reagan
was able to once again shift the secrecy balance in favor of
the executive. His "remarkable success" in relations with
the media[89] as well as his high popularity ratings created
a new level of trust which had not been seen in some time.
In 1982, President Reagan signed Executive Order 12,065
which greatly increased the quantity of information which
could be classified.[90] The Pentagon's secret budget
requests rose from $5.5 billion in fiscal year 1981 to $24.3
billion in fiscal year 1988. Some congressional calls for
the disclosure of military secrets to Congress came in the
wake of these increases in the percentage of defense
spending held under the cover of secrecy. For example, in
1987 two bills were introduced into the House which aimed at
allowing members of Congress to know more about secret
defense spending.[91]

When the focus of this investigation is shifted to
the case study of the Strategic Defense Initiative, it will
become evident that the secrecy balance played an important

---

[88] Raymond Hutchings, Soviet Secrecy and Non-Secrecy
(Totowa, New Jersey: Barnes & Noble Books, 1988), 226.

[89] Carnes Lord, The Presidency and the Management of
National Security (New York: The Free Press, 1988), 8.

[90] 3 C.F.R. 166 (1982).

[91] David C. Morrison, "Dancing in the Dark." National
Journal 11 April 1987: 867-868.

role in maintaining congressional support for the weapon system. When the Iran-Contra Affair subsequently occurred, the balance was again shifted toward the legislative branch. One conclusion scholars have reached from the proceedings of the Iran-Contra hearings is that the executive branch applies information restrictions to many details which need not be classified. The later declassification of many key elements of SDI (which came in part as a repercussion of Iran-Contra) had a tremendous political effect on support for that program.

Public vs. Congressional Access:
Limited Distinction Due to Narrow Interest

During the early years of the Cold War, Congress was often denied information on the basis of laws which it had itself passed. One law which induced this problem was the Atomic Energy Act of 1946 which restricted the dissemination of information regarding nuclear weapons. This and other statutory references were cited by the executive branch as reasons for denying congressional information requests. On October 31, 1951, Congress attempted to counter this problem by enacting a statute relating to the disclosure of classified information. This law included a clause which guaranteed that disclosure laws could not be used as a justification for denying congressional committees defense information.[92] While the issue remained far from resolved, this act insured that Congress would not handcuff itself in attempts to gain information. Today, executive agencies may not use laws that prevent public access to information as a basis for preventing congressional access.

The legal citation mentioned above may seem to provide an open channel through which Congress may receive unlimited information. In theory, this statute enabled Congress to limit the use of disclosure laws as a means of preventing its members from receiving classified information. However, this law would only come to affect information which was specifically requested. The realities of congressional operations usually prevent individual members from requesting information on a regular basis. For this reason, the distinction between public and congressional information is often found to be so small that it is insignificant.

In many ways, the distinction between releasing information to Congress and releasing it to the public is very limited. The ability to discuss a topic in open session might make the matter of greater interest to the average member of Congress. From a practical perspective, results of a discussion held in closed session are irrelevant to most of a member's constituents. As a result,

---

[92]   18 U.S.C., Sec. 798(c) (1951).

a representative will receive no credit for considering this seemingly inconsequential issue. Time spent on such secret legislative work represents time which a legislator could have spent on issues of relevance to that member's district. Popular opinion and public image are important forces which often direct congressional decision making. Classified information, although factual and relevant, is likely to play a secondary role in the decision making process for most members.

There are other reasons why the question of public access to information is not totally separate from that of Congressional access. Giving a member of Congress and his or her immediate staff access to national security secrets might enhance Congressional understanding of the matter. Practically speaking, however, members and their staffs will be unable to give thorough consideration to these issues. In many policy areas, this thorough consideration is conducted within research institutes, academic institutions and scholarly journals. For example, many members pay special attention to the work of various think tanks in Washington such as the Brookings Institution and the Center for Strategic and International Studies. Preventing these institutions from obtaining the information they need to reach conscientious determinations concerning an issue might in effect damage Congress' ability to obtain their professional conclusion.

Preventing outside groups from drawing conclusions on classified information often causes defense information to be ignored. When situations arise where secrecy prevents members from giving thorough consideration to an issue, some use this as an opportunity to take a much needed break. Members of Congress often find no time in their schedules for the pursuit of such seemingly optional activities as obtaining classified information. The 94th Congress established the Obey Commission to recommend ways in which members of Congress might reduce their work pressures and improve their scheduling. The Commission found that an average member of Congress works eleven hours a day and has a schedule which is, "long, fragmented, and unpredictable."[93] In light of these existing time constraints, a member of Congress is taking on an ambitious project when he or she allocates additional hours toward the pursuit of classified information. The limited political payoff for such involvement keeps the number of members who are willing to accept this challenge at a minimum.

---

[93]   Anthony King, ed., The New American Political System (Washington, D.C.: American Enterprise Institute, 1978), 160.

Congressional Leaks as a Political Device

The process of leaking information is one option members of Congress have by which they might make a classified matter public. Intentional leaks are most often conducted in an attempt to affect a certain policy outcome. They are often undertaken in situations where the desired policy outcome may not be affected by conventional public policy methods. In the legislative rebuttal to the executive's national security argument, however, we found that members of Congress might be held liable for such leaks. In almost every situation, the benefits of illegally revealing classified information are less than the punitive costs. For this reason, leaks are most often conducted on an anonymous basis.

Research for this study has shown that the number of anonymous congressional leaks regarding classified defense information is negligible. It is true that congressional leaks may be used as potent political devices. Whereas the precedent for anonymously leaking defense secrets is minimal, however, the subject warrants little discussion in this report. Generally speaking, the practice of making anonymous disclosures has come under serious criticism in recent times. Statements made by unnamed sources usually carry less force than those of open attestants since these assertions are not easily checked. Such a source prevents the motives of the statement from being examined and effectively denies any further solicitation of background information. In carrying out an anonymous leak of classified material, a government official might be seen as failing to comply with his or her moral obligations to the public.[94] Whereas defense secrets are protected by law, anonymously leaking these materials may be found to be even more unconscionable.

The potential problem of congressional leaks has constituted a major reason why the executive branch is unwilling to share information with Congress. The problem of information leaks *by members of* Congress might be protected against by drafting stricter penalties for such offenses. Making all members of Congress subject to the same set of strict rules applicable to the members of the Select Intelligence Committee would be one method of implementing such restrictions.[95] Another would be to prosecute members under the same statutes that executive employees are held accountable to.

---

[94]   Joel L. Fleishman, Lance Liebman, and Mark H. Moore, eds., Public Duties: The Moral Obligations of Government Officials (Cambridge, Massachusetts: Harvard University Press, 1981), 212.

[95]   Harold Hongju Koh, The National Security Constitution: Sharing Power after the Iran Contra Affair (New Haven, Connecticut: Yale University Press, 1990), 117.

Excessive Classification: A Legitimate
Overexpansion of Executive Power

Earlier, it was suggested that Congress might limit
the classification power of the executive to the following
categories of information: technicalities of weapon systems,
plans for military operations, details of diplomatic
negotiations, and intelligence procedures. This argument
was used as a basis for our analysis of congressional claims
to information. Although the restrictions on the authority
of the executive found in this theory are rather narrow,
they leave open a tremendous window for excessive
classification. Despite this fact, current laws regarding
government secrecy include far fewer restrictions than those
suggested in our original model.

The Department of Defense enjoys considerable
flexibility in determining what and how much information it
wishes to classify. At times, the quantity of information
which is held under classification restrictions has been
called into question. Some members of Congress consider
overclassification to be one of the most serious offenses of
the executive's power to withhold secret information.
Former Senate Appropriations Defense Subcommittee member
Lowell P. Weicker, Jr. (R-CT) believed that the upward trend
of secret spending is due in large part to the rise of
stealth technology. It is his fear that as this type of

technology continues to grow, the percentage of the defense
budget which is kept secret will reach an unconscionable
level.[96]

In an attempt to justify what might be considered
an abuse of power, the Pentagon has stated that the main
reason for such overclassification is that, "The nature and
magnitude of [Defense Department] operations often
necessitates a less-than-rigorous application of the
[standard] need-to-know principle [to classified
programs]."[97] One solution to this problem would be to
allocate more funds to programs which would facilitate
declassification. Responsibility for the appropriation of
such fund rests in the hands of the Congress. If Congress
refuses to allocate such funds, the executive might shift
the blame for resulting problems onto the legislative
branch.

The quantity of information which the executive
chooses to classify is itself a political question. From a
practical standpoint, it is often in the best interest of
the executive to declassify information if there is no
reason to prevent disclosure. Openness in government is
typically viewed as a virtue of the democratic model for
government. Exposing classified information allows the

---

[96]   David C. Morrison, "Dancing in the Dark." National
Journal 11 April 1987: 872.

[97]   David C. Morrison, "Dancing in the Dark." National
Journal 11 April 1987: 869.

legislative branch to check the executive's power and allows the public to fully consider the current issues of the nation. The president may relieve himself of skepticism and even criticism by keeping classification levels at a minimum. Congress' power to appropriate funds provides another strong enticement for cooperation.

From the opposite standpoint, the executive may also choose to keep a great deal of information classified. From a management standpoint, the President may find this highly advantageous. Within the executive branch, the president may be able to increase his power by maintaining strong control of the federal bureaucracy. If levels of secrecy reach an excessive degree, however, the executive branch provides Congress with an invitation for conflict. Secrecy diminishes the Congress' power to oversee the executive branch. When this situation receives the attention of a significant percentage of Congress, the executive's political power will most likely be challenged. When the executive branch possesses information which it does not want to release, it may deny disclosure. Historically, such refusals often escalate into fervent political battles. This type of confrontation usually leads to a shift of the secrecy balance in favor of the legislative branch.

Ambiguities and Other Deficiencies in the Law:
An Initiation for Heavy Executive Control

Earlier, the vagueness of the term national security was discussed as it applied to the debate over secrecy. There is a direct relationship between the lack of a precise definition for this term and the ambiguity in the laws which delineate the methods by which information will be classified. The result is tremendous executive flexibility in the realm of secrecy.

Many acts of Congress which were created for the increase of public access to information have exemptions for data on national security. In 1966, the Freedom of Information Act was passed in order, "to ensure an informed citizenry, vital to the functioning of a democratic society, needed to check against corruption and to hold the governors accountable to the governors."[98] Between 1972 and 1976, Congress also passed the Federal Advisory Committee Act, the Privacy Act and the Government in the Sunshine Act.[99] It must be noted, however, that each of these statutes include

---

[98] U.S. Library of Congress, Congressional Research Service, The Application of the Freedom of Information Act to Congress: A Legal Analysis, by Jay Shampansky, April 28, 1992, CRS Report 92-403 A, 2.

[99] U.S. Library of Congress, Congressional Research Service, Access to Government Information in the United States, by Harold C. Relyea, September 25, 1991, CRS Report 91-697 GOV, 3.

significant exemptions to the rule of access. For example, one exemption of the Freedom of Information Act "permits the withholding of properly classified documents. Information may be classified in the interest of national defense or foreign policy."[100] Legislative proposals aimed at constraining the executive's definition of national security have found little support in either house.

Inadequate means of regulating executive classification authority have been matched by insufficient procedures for requiring the president to provide information. In 1974, Senator Charles Mathias (R-MD) stated:

> Congressional efforts to compel Executive compliance with its requests have generally failed primarily because the means of compulsion at the disposal of the Congress are so crude as to be virtually unemployable and also because, in what is essentially a boundary dispute the courts have never ruled upon, the Executive has successfully ignored Congressional efforts at compulsion.[101]

---

[100] U.S. Congress, House, Committee on Government Operations, A Citizen's Guide on Using the Freedom of Information Act and the Privacy Act of 1974 to Request Government Records, Report, 102d Cong., 1st Sess. Washington, D.C.: GPO, 1991, 12.

[101] Thomas M. Franck and Edward Weisband, eds., Secrecy and Foreign Policy (New York: Oxford University Press, 1974), 81.

When the problem is viewed from a strictly legal
perspective, it is true that the methods of requiring the
executive to provide information are crude. One critic
summarized the legal procedures available to the legislative
branch as follows.

> Congress undoubtedly has power to punish contempts
> without invoking the aid of the executive and the
> judiciary, by the simple forthright process of
> causing the Sergeant at Arms to seize the offender
> and clap him in the common jail of the District of
> Columbia or the guardroom of the Capitol
> Police.[102]

The Congress often finds it difficult to firmly press
members of the executive branch to release information.
Fortunately, however, it may compel the executive to comply
without carrying out or even threatening such severe actions
as the one described above. The most effective way of
carrying this out would come through applying political
pressure on the executive to do such. These political
methods will be demonstrated in our Case Study of SDI.

---

[102]   Joseph W. Bishop, Jr., "The Executive Right of
Privacy: An Unresolved Constitutional Question," Yale Law
Journal 66 (1957): 484.

Obstacles to Congressional Legal Action

Most members of Congress would agree that keeping secrets regarding national defense technology from our rivals is in the best interest of U.S. national security. However, bills which require the executive branch to reveal the existence of black programs most often fail to become law due to a different concern. Many legislators are more concerned with the protection of intelligence programs and covert operations. It is feared that creating comprehensive rules for information disclosure would impinge on the integrity of these delicate areas.

Some suggest that Congress must be the body that ultimately decides whether the disclosure risk is greater than Congress' need for information.[103] However, even if such a system were instituted, citing this balance is often a difficult point to establish. One member's need for information will not be perceived identically throughout the legislature. Many controversies over defense information often receive heavy media attention and then die suddenly. In such instances, either a member or a small group of members band together to protest a lack of openness. Soon

-----

[103] Paul C. Rosenthal and Robert S. Grossman, "Congressional Access to Confidential Information Collected by Federal Agencies," Harvard Journal on Legislation 15 (1977): 77.

thereafter, the matter will be forgotten when not enough members can be gathered to challenge the entire executive branch.

Finally, congressional action must be viewed in the context of the power struggle between governmental branches. It has been suggested that the three central reasons why the president has most often won in the effort to rule in foreign policy matters are presidential initiative, congressional acquiescence, and judicial tolerance.[104] This argument runs parallel to the reasons why Congress has not been able to attach a permanent equilibrium point to the secrecy balance. Presidential initiative regarding the issue of secrecy is intrinsic to the executive's position in that classified information originates in the executive branch. For this reason, critics believe that the executive holds an unfair advantage in this political struggle. Congressional acquiescence on matters concealed in secrecy was earlier attributed to the fact that issues addressed in closed session are unrewarded by constituents. Judicial tolerance has been based on the political nature of secrecy.

---

[104] Harold Hongju Koh, The National Security Constitution: Sharing Power after the Iran Contra Affair (New Haven, Connecticut: Yale University Press, 1990), 117.

Verdict From the Judicial Branch:
Secrecy is a Political Question

When the disputes between the two branches are analyzed from a legal standpoint, it becomes apparent that the issue is often highly political. While the sheer forces of law may be felt to some extent within this struggle, the final outcome is most often one which is based on politics. The courts have repeatedly refused to hear cases concerning restrictions on secrecy due to these very reasons. It is obvious that litigating a matter where the balance between executive and congressional powers are in question is a painful task. Such trials create a burdensome drain on the resources of each party. Objections to increasing the level of codified mandates for the disclosure of executive information have often been based on fears that such matters would occupy court time with what is largely a political issue. The best scenario would be one in which an agreement could be reached between the two branches over a formula for information release. In most cases, a different formula exists for each scenario.

When considering the need for information in Congressional decision-making, it is also important to balance the effect of information disclosure on presidential decision-making. However, from a legal standpoint courts

have often decided that protecting the integrity of the
decision-making process alone does not provide enough reason
to withhold information from Congress.

Some have suggested that the final decision in the
A.T.&T. case serve as an example for judicial intervention
in future disputes over the balance between executive
secrecy and congressional needs. In this case. the court
refused to act as a final arbiter and instead chose to "act
as an overseer of settlement negotiations."[105] As we shift
our focus to our case study of the Strategic Defense
Initiative, we will find that the courts often refuse to
even go this far.

A CASE STUDY OF THE STRATEGIC DEFENSE INITIATIVE

In a March 9, 1992 opinion piece in the Washington
Post, Aldric Saucier stated that the progress of the SDI
program had been a result of the, "substitution of political
science for the scientific method."[106] His comment was
not intended to compliment the public policy methods used by
the staff working on the project. On the contrary, it was

---

[105]   U.S. Library of Congress, Congressional Research
Service, Congressional Access To Information From the
Executive: A Legal Analysis, by Richard Ehlke, March 10,
1986, CRS Report 86-50 A, 17.

[106]   Aldric Saucier, "Lost in Space," New York Times, 9
March 1992, A17.

an indictment of several partisan activities taken by administrators of SDI. Mr. Saucier claimed that many of these managers had corruptly misrepresented the scientific progress of the program for political purposes. Ten years after its inception, the Strategic Defense Initiative's completion is stalled by a lack of numerous scientific elements which have yet to be developed. Nonetheless, several political developments involving this program make it an excellent case study for our investigation of secrecy.

Our investigation of the Strategic Defense Initiative will address the question of secrecy from two main perspectives. The first involves the results of secrecy. Here we will consider how secrecy changes the overall balance of power in the political arena. This study will discuss four main hypotheses.

Hypothesis 1: Public exposure of key facts may lead to strategic shifts in policy.

Hypothesis 2: The results of scientific tests may be used as potent political tools.

Hypothesis 3: Secrecy may be used as a marketing tactic.

Hypothesis 4: Inexplicit appropriations by
Congress may be used to increase
subsidies.

.

A thorough discussion of these results will prove
that secrecy is a substantial section of power. Once this
has been proven, it will become important to note how this
element of power may be shifted in favor of either the
Congress or the president. This will become the focus of
our second level of analysis. As a result of our study,
three methods of changing the balance of secrecy have been
developed. They are as follows:

Change 1: Corruption may decrease an
executive's claim to information

Change 2: Serious requests for classified
information may prove congressional
needs for such materials.

Change 3: The judicial branch plays a limited
role in changing the secrecy
balance.

Public Exposure of Key Facts May
Lead to Strategic Shifts in Policy

The history of the balance of secrecy displays a number of occasions when the location of the balance rested firmly in the favor of the executive branch. The two terms of the Reagan Administration represented just such an occasion. As was mentioned earlier, Reagan enacted Executive Order 12,065 which greatly increased his information classification authority. In addition, the Pentagon's secret budget requests quadrupled during his administration. Finally, President Reagan was able to exercise more control over national security information as a result of legislative restructuring. Many committees which had been created in the previous era of reform were later terminated in an effort to streamline the work of Congress. These developments came as a disappointment to those who favored the relative openness of the previous administrations.[107]

In March 1983, President Reagan announced the beginning of the Strategic Defense Initiative. From its

---

[107] John M. Oseth, Regulating U.S. Intelligence Operations: A Study in Definition of the National Interest (Lexington, Kentucky: University Press of Kentucky, 1985), 160.

inception, this program would be one of great controversy. Much of the protest against the SDI was based on the grounds that the system would never work.

In an elaborate discussion of multiple target tracking, Jeffrey Uhlmann described the problems involved with using SDI for a full-scale nuclear attack. Mr. Uhlmann, a computer scientist from the Naval Research Lab in Washington, explained that:

> If tracking a single baseball or warhead or missile requires a certain measurable level of effort, then it might seem that tracking 10 similar objects would require at most 10 times as much effort. Actually, for the most obvious methods of solving the problem, the difficulty is proportional to the square of the number of objects; thus 10 objects demand 100 times the effort, and 10,000 objects increase the difficulty to a factor of 100 million.[108]

For years this provided a crux in the argument against ballistic missile defenses. The complex nature of numerous-target scenarios left President Reagan's grand vision for an impenetrable shield in question.

---

[108] Jeffrey K.Uhlmann, "Algorithms for Multiple-Target Tracking," American Scientist 80 (March-April 1992): 128.

Even those who suspected that SDI would work remained suspicious on the grounds that partial success of an operational system would be equivalent to complete failure. The massive capability for destruction which nuclear weapons hold would make the penetration of only one weapon entirely unacceptable. Opponents felt that SDI would provide a false sense of security. For this reason alone, many did not find a need for further information.

Many individuals in Congress and the public had resolved to stand in opposition of the program regardless of its technical feasibility. To these critics, the Star Wars system would provide, "fundamental challenges to deterrence and arms control," regardless of whether it became operational or not.[109] There were fears that SDI could be employed for offensive military efforts. The system, when fully developed, might be used to take out an enemy's early-warning satellites and communications. Additionally, it would allow one side to hold a first strike capability as well as a shield against retaliation.[110] Such a scenario would effectively tilt the delicate nuclear arms balance in one nation's favor, leaving international security in jeopardy. The very premises upon which detente was based

---

[109] John Tirman, Sovereign Acts: American Unilateralism and Global Security (New York: Harper & Row Publishers, 1989), 9.

[110] William J. Broad, "Serious Sharing of 'Star Wars?' Not in This Millennium," New York Times, February 23, 1992, Sect. 4, 5.

would be acutely imperiled.

Others believed that a U.S. strategic defense system would actually provide the Soviet Union with an incentive to "go first" if a nuclear conflict appeared near. If SDI did in fact have serious vulnerabilities, an attack made when the Soviets were at full strength would most effectively exploit those vulnerabilities by actively overloading the system.[111]

The goal of achieving a comprehensive defense against a large-scale nuclear attack remained alive throughout the Reagan Administration. In his annual report for FY1988, Secretary of Defense Caspar Weinberger stated that the main objective of SDI was to "secure a thoroughly reliable defense against Soviet nuclear missiles to protect all our people."[112] Soon thereafter, however, information was released which brought this goal into serious question.

In the late 1980's and early 1990's, technological facts surrounding the program were released to the press by those who worked on the program. These leaks of classified information showed fundamental problems in the program which made Reagan's vision for a global defense seem highly

---

[111] John Tirman, Sovereign Acts: American Unilateralism and Global Security (New York: Harper & Row Publishers, 1989), 68.

[112] Daniel Wirls, Buildup: The Politics of Defense in the Reagan Era (Ithaca, New York: Cornell University Press, 1992), 156.

unrealistic. These developments reduced public and congressional support for the SDI program. In order for SDI to stay alive, it became apparent that fundamental changes in policy would have to occur.

The Strategic Defense Initiative Organization (SDIO) described the Missile Defense Act of 1991 as a "basis for a new consensus between the Administration and Congress."[113] This act refocused the strategy of SDI from one that emphasized global defense to one which focused on theater defenses. Essentially, the Scud Missile attacks of the Persian Gulf War demonstrated a newly emerging threat. SDI was well positioned to take on this challenge. As one *congressional aide put it*, "The TV images of the Patriot were worth $1 Billion to SDI."[114] Ironically, the Army's claims of Patriot Missile success would also receive intensive questioning later on. Although earlier claims put its interception rate as high as eighty percent, that figure was later reduced significantly.[115]

Had the information concerning the slow rate of progress been available to Congress at an earlier point in time, SDI might have evolved quite differently. Initial

[113]   David C. Morrison, "Missile Defenses: More Debate." National Journal, 8 February 1992: 337.

[114]   David A. Kaplan, "A Safety Net Full of Holes," Newsweek, 23 March 1992, 59.

[115]   Eric Schmitt, "Democratic Senators Challenging Cost and Risk of 'Star Wars' Plan," New York Times, 10 April 1992, A25.

disclosure of this information would have catalyzed this shift in spending and strategic change in policy. Although the end of the Cold War brought about a critical shift in the international security environment, it is politically unrealistic to believe that this represented the only reason for SDI's change in strategy.

The Results of Scientific Tests May
Be Used as Potent Political Tools

Representatives of the Department of Defense often testify before congressional committees regarding weapons acquisition programs. The level of funding which will be allocated toward a particular system is quite often based on the level of progress which the associated defense contractors have been able to maintain. Such progress may be well certified by providing the results of testing. If the tests prove that the system's performance is showing significant deficiencies in terms of predicted time, cost or quality, the justification for continued funding of that program will be thoroughly questioned.[116]

On March 17, 1992, a DOD official disclosed the

---

[116]   Merton J. Peck and Frederic M. Scherer, The Weapons Acquisition Process: An Economic Analysis (Boston: Harvard University Graduate School of Business Administration, 1962), 543.

negative results of an SDI test held in the Pacific Ocean.
During this test, a ground based rocket was unable to
intercept a simulated enemy missile. Although the test was
secret, the information concerning the outcome was leaked to
the press by an anonymous Pentagon source.[117] The
political repercussions of this release had the potential to
become quite serious. The Bush Administration had recently
requested a large increase in SDI spending for the following
fiscal year. Although this test might have prevented
congressional decision makers from granting the Bush
request, it did not lead to a cut in spending. That year,
congressional appropriations for SDI showed little change
from the year before.

Another result of recent testing was an exposure of
significant command and control problems within the program.
While much of the system is automated, U.S. commanders would
be engaged in coordinating defensive efforts. Simulations
of combat scenarios have proven that these commanders would
be overloaded during an actual missile strike.[118]

In many cases, secrecy leads critics to assume the
worst case scenario. In a comprehensive General Accounting
Office (GAO) study of SDI, analysts found nothing to prove

---

[117]   Associated Press, "U.S. Says Rocket Failed to
Destroy Mock Warhead in Pacific Test," New York Times, 18
March 1992, B6.

[118]   Vincent Kiernan, "Simulations Change SDI
Thinking," Space News, 20 April 1992, 7.

that the "tremendous technological challenges," confronting
the project were anywhere near solution. While the Pentagon
objected to this judgment, the GAO retorted that no
"convincing evidence " had been supplied by DOD which would
lead them to conclude otherwise.[119] Scientific testing
might be used to create such evidence.

The results of weapons trials were especially
important in the case of SDI. Many weapons systems which
are developed eventually become operational. In the case of
SDI, skeptics fear that this will never happen. Richard
Garwin, a physicist from IBM went so far as to claim that
the plans for SDI under the original global strategy,
"defied the laws of physics."[120] Weapons testing may be
used to disprove such assertions.

As was discussed earlier, post-Cold War realities
have changed the way policy makers look at SDI. This is
especially true on Capitol Hill. While the scare of an all
out nuclear war has largely subsided, SDI now might not be
expected to demobilize a volley of 100 or more missiles.
Accidental launches, terrorist actions or third world
offensive efforts would not result in any more than a few
fired weapons. Sidney Drell, a Stanford physicist and past
opponent of SDI, stated last year that large scale

---

[119]   George Lardner, "'Star Wars' Plan Invites
Problems, GAO Warns," Washington Post, 11 March 1992, A7.

[120]   David A. Kaplan, "A Safety Net Full of Holes,"
Newsweek, 23 March 1992, 56.

reductions in the world arsenal of ballistic missiles would allay, "concerns about SDI deployments and their threat to stability."[121]

Whereas it is now more conceivable that a limited defensive system would be adequate, technological aspects including the results of scientific testing have become of greater interest to decision-makers. A representative that was steadfastly against a strategy of SDI in the past might now have a greater interest in the details and therefore require additional information.

Beyond the final stage of laboratory experimentation, members of Congress appreciate evaluations of operational performance in the battlefield. For example, the Persian Gulf War proved the ability of the turbine-powered M1 Abrams tank to perform effectively for prolonged periods in a harsh environment without losing its effectiveness.[122] With such concrete evidence of the system's capabilities, proponents for the project hold a strong justification for a continuation of procurement.

The lack of battlefield test results often represents a major obstacle to the continuation of a weapons project. Due to the importance of the results of such tests

---

[121]   Jay P. Kosminsky, ed., "SDI Issues Update," The SDI Report, 15 January 1992, 2.

[122]   Les Aspin and William Dickinson, Defense for a New Era: Lessons of the Persian Gulf War (Washington, D.C.: U.S. Government Printing Office, 1992), 17.

in congressional decision making, opponents of SDI will always hold a compelling argument against this program. In the case of this system, scientists will never be unable to fully test its operational effectiveness unless the United States is attacked by ballistic missiles. Members of Congress do not require an advanced technical understanding of SDI to realize this simple reality. For these reasons, secrecy has become less of an issue.

Secrecy May Be Used as a Marketing Tactic

Elliott Kennel, a physicist who worked on SDI during the 1980's said, "If you keep all the technical data under wraps, it's easy to keep it funded."[123] Some claim that the positive results of SDI development which were often shown to Congress during the 1980's showed only part of the story. There is now sufficient proof that the strategic disclosure and withholding of information has been used as an efficacious marketing tactic throughout the development of SDI.

In most cases the burden of proof is on the executive branch. SDI researchers might be able to develop a method for overcoming various technical obstacles. In

---

[123]   David A. Kaplan, "A Safety Net Full of Holes," Newsweek, 23 March 1992, 57.

order to gain congressional support for SDI, certain classified information must be released to Congress. Until then, negative perceptions will prevail. For example, major outside studies have concluded that a completed Star Wars system costing a total of $1.37 trillion would allow two to ten percent of an enemy's missiles through its protective shield.[124]

Budget requests must be calculated so that both the rate of development and the yearly cost are each factored. In an effort to show the desired final results of the SDI program, Bush Administration officials had considered requesting extra funds. One expert believed that if such a move were taken, Congress would have, "move[d] to cut out or sharply reduce space-based funding."[125]

Inexplicit Appropriations by Congress
May Be Used to Increase Subsidies

In some ways, the veil of secrecy allowed SDI research to expand beyond the level which was officially recognized by the Congress. Since the 1960's, the United States has been developing anti-satellite (ASAT) weapons.

---

[124] Aldric Saucier, "Lost in Space," New York Times, 9 March 1992, A17.

[125] David C. Morrison, "Missile Defenses: More Debate." National Journal, 8 February 1992: 337.

These systems could be used to destroy an enemy's ability to observe U.S. force composition and movement following the commencement of conflict. Over the last thirty years, the Air Force has conducted significant testing and development of such weapons.[126] Similarly, early SDI research was promoted as a means of fostering the development of space surveillance techniques. Such surveillance is a necessary component which would be used to track enemy missiles before intercept.[127]

According to some analysts, the veil of secrecy has allowed some SDI research to be undertaken as part of ASAT development. Whereas much of the technology of these two programs is highly interrelated, congressional support for the ASAT program has inadvertently lead to precipitated development of SDI. This relationship was researched intensively by several members of Congress and their staffs during the late eighties. Such investigations allowed members to understand this hidden connection and consequently limit ASAT development.[128]

---

[126] Joseph S. Nye, Jr. and James A. Schear, eds., Seeking Stability in Space: Anti-Satellite Weapons and the Evolving Space Regime (Lanham, Maryland: University Press of America, 1987), 9.

[127] William E. Burrows, Deep Black: Space Espionage and National Security (New York: Random House, 1986), 310.

[128] John Tirman, Sovereign Acts: American Unilateralism and Global Security (New York: Harper & Row Publishers, 1989), 45.

Another example of SDI's development of a wide base of support came when Navy involvement in the program was initiated. Basing the program around the already developed Standard Missile system, Congress authorized $90 million to be spent on equipping a number of US Navy Aegis ships for theater defenses.[129] These ships would be used to test and later deploy the newly developed Ground Based Interceptors (GBI's). This program was begun at a time when many members of Congress had become increasingly indignant over high SDI funding.

The $90 million specifically allocated towards this program does not represent a comprehensive accounting of the total cost of implementing this plan. Various additional expenses must be included when deriving this aggregate sum including the operational costs of the ship as well as personnel costs. For example, a Ticonderoga-class cruiser has a total manning of 24 officers and 340 enlisted. The unit cost of each of these ships is $884.4 million in FY1989 dollars.[130] The 364 men on board each ship represent personnel that would have been financed by SDI funds if these tests were conducted on land. If the average life span of these cruisers is assumed to be 30 years, each year

---

[129] Barbara Starr, "SDI Funds Sought for Aegis Ships," Jane's Defence Weekly, 21 November 1992, 13.

[130] Norman Polmar, The Ships and Aircraft of the U.S. Fleet, 14th ed. (Annapolis, Maryland: Naval Institute Press, 1987), 112-113.

of operation represents nearly $30 million of the original cost of the ship. SDI funding does not compensate for these expenses. As a result, the amount spent on SDI programs is actually substantially higher than the official aggregate which is promulgated to members of Congress.

From a political standpoint, it might be noted that the naval support of SDI funding also represents a means for gaining wider support on Capitol Hill. With force cuts imminent, finding a justification for keeping naval operational units afloat is a key concern of interested members of Congress. To many, these SDI tests represent a valid grounds for obtaining that support. Senator John Warner (R-VA) and Congressman Norm Sisisky (D-VA) each represent the area surrounding the Norfolk naval base which serves as a home port to a large number of these Ticonderoga-class cruisers. Coincidentally, both of these members serve on the armed services committee of their respective house. To them, support for SDI now represents support for this navy program which in turn translates into constituent support. If congressional decision making is viewed from a broad perspective, it becomes apparent why such logic might play an important role in a member's final determination on an issue. For most, these political considerations vastly outweigh any knowledge which might be derived from a comprehensive review of classified information on the SDI program.

Changes in the Secrecy Balance

Each of our four hypotheses have helped to prove the political nature of the question of secrecy. Having made this essential distinction, we may now consider how this element of the overall power equation may be shifted in favor of either the Congress or the president. The four hypotheses provided above have formed the basis for our second level of analysis. This second section of investigation within our case study of SDI lead to the development of three methods of changing the balance of secrecy.

Corruption May Decrease an
Executive's Claim to Information

Congress is much less likely to request secret information from federal agencies which have proven themselves to run in a veracious manner. Much of Congress' recent call for openness in the SDI program may be attributed to the malpractices in the project which were exposed by Aldric Saucier.

At times, technical secrecy cannot effectively conceal mismanagement within a weapons program. One way the barrier may be broken is through obtaining an inside perspective from a member of the executive branch. While an

official may not be constricted from revealing specifics,
prevailing deficiencies may be indicated legally. On
February 14, 1992, a scientist working on the SDI project
met with a number of congressional aides. Aldric Saucier
openly cooperated with the staffers' investigation of SDI,
as he acknowledged technical deficiencies and, "incoherent
and fragmented management". Later that same day, Saucier
was fired by SDIO. "Unacceptable performance," was cited as
the justification for his dismissal.[131]

The government's Office of Special Counsel,
ordered Secretary of Defense Richard B. Cheney to
investigate Saucier's allegations. Issuing a directive on
February 27, 1992, the office found a "substantial
likelihood" in the scientist's claims. The directive also
required an investigation into related charges which could
be even more detrimental to future funding for SDI. These
included complaints that the office had mislead Congress and
had falsified expenditure records.[132] Also, a Lieutenant
General was accused of making, "improperly inflated claims
of efficacy of a "Star Wars" program.[133]

Senator David Pryor, chairman of the Senate

[131]   Rodrigo Lazo, "Whistleblower Fired From Star Wars
Staff," Federal Times, 2 March 1992, 5.

[132]   George Lardner, "Cheney Told to Probe Scientist's
Charge of Misconduct, Waste by SDI Officials," Washington
Post, 2 March 1992, A5.

[133]   John H. Cushman, Jr., "Whistleblower Wins Study of
'Star Wars' Program," New York Times, 3 March 1992, A13.

Governmental Affairs subcommittee on federal services,
described the secretive SDIO as, "an invisible bureaucracy
of contractors feeding from the open money sack." However,
information restrictions did not prevent him from uncovering
a number of management inefficiencies within the office.
Many contracts granted excessive management responsibility
to private firms, thereby limiting DOD control over certain
projects. In addition, Pryor provided evidence that SDIO
had recently spent $166,000 on trips to such sites as
Honolulu, Orlando and San Diego.[134]

The Saucier affair and the incident described above
each created momentum in Congress which allowed them to
shift the secrecy balance in their favor. As a standard for
comparison, the Iran-Contra affair uncovered problems
created by excessive secrecy in the executive branch. As a
result of these abuses, Congress began to probe more deeply
into covert operations. Similarly, the incidents discussed
in this segment of our case study lead Congress to request
more thorough information on the internal management of the
Strategic Defense Initiative.

---

[134]   George Lardner, "Pryor Says SDI Is Tainted by
Contractors," Washington Post, 28 February 1992, A21.

Significant Requests For Classified Information May
Prove Congressional Needs For Such Materials

When a member of Congress publicly speaks out
against the information restrictions of the executive
branch, that member most often finds only minimal support
from his or her colleagues. Although such public statements
are quite common, they usually lack the critical mass which
is necessary to take on the executive branch of government.
It may be found that this critical mass might be developed
in a number of ways. First, members of Congress might show
a greater interest in obtaining classified information.
Second, members of the congressional leadership may use
their considerable political power to pressure the executive
in releasing information. Thirdly, a large number of
members of Congress may join together in making an
information request.

The executive derives significant power from
Congress' lack of interest in classified information. Very
seldom does a member of Congress exercise his or her right
to review classified material held by the Armed Services
Committees of the U.S. Congress. It is quite easy for a
member to check out and review records of the classified
testimony which is held in executive session. These
testimonies provide succinct summaries of key legislative

issues. Nonetheless, on the average, less than a dozen members examine these materials each year. Within the past six months, not one member has requested classified information concerning SDI. With this fact in mind, it is hard to justify a need for information which is much more specific and much less comprehensible.

SDI was the battleground for an intense political battle in 1992. Senate Majority Leader Mitchell called for $15 million in cuts from the program over five years in a January 16 speech at the National Press Club.[135] Had these remarks come from a less senior senator, they might not receive the same level of notice from the executive. President Bush's consistent promotion of the program throughout this volley of attacks showed significant resolve in light of forceful congressional efforts made to limit spending.

The outrage over the Saucier incident lead numerous members of Congress, including Senate Majority Leader George Mitchell and Senator William Cohen, to voice vehement protests against the action. As a result, the scientist was placed back on the Pentagon payroll until the matter could be fully investigated.[136] When numerous members band together in a coalition, they hold a much more viable method

---

[135]   Jay P. Kosminsky, ed., "SDI Issues Update," The SDI Report, 20 February 1992, 2.

[136]   George Lardner, "SDI Scientist Wins Reprieve From Firing," Washington Post, 7 March 1992, A8.

for challenging the executive branch. The senior status of Senator Mitchell also added to the political power of the coalition.

The Judicial Branch Plays a Limited Role in Changing the Secrecy Balance

As was stated before, the political nature of the balance of secrecy makes it an issue that has received little attention from the courts. The court has repeatedly refused to hear cases concerning this matter on these grounds. *This point is supported by the history of SDI.* Not one case has been brought to any court over the question of the balance of secrecy between the Congress and the executive branch of government with regards to SDI. This non-involvement follows the model set forth by the A.T. & T. case by which the court refuses to act as a final arbiter in decisions concerning secrecy. Instead, the struggle has been handled directly by the executive and legislative branches of government.

CONCLUSION

In the preliminary segments of this investigation, the commonly accepted explanations for the position of the secrecy balance were significantly discredited. In the first section, the element of national security was considered as the executive's justification for withholding information. Next, the legal arguments used to justify information disclosures were examined. Each of these elements were found to have only a slight effect on the contemporary secrecy balance. Instead, secrecy was found to be a political question which has variably shifted in favor of the Congress and the Executive throughout American history.

Once the question of secrecy was determined to be a political question, it was possible to place it into the context of the political struggle over SDI. This case study allowed us to examine secrecy on two separate levels. In the first segment, we questioned the way secrecy may change the overall balance of power in the political arena. Here we found that public exposure of key facts may lead to strategic shifts in policy. It was also determined that the results of scientific tests may be used as potent political tools. Next, secrecy was found to be used as a marketing tactic. Finally, inexplicit appropriations by Congress were determined to be one means of increasing subsidies.

Having determined that secrecy was an important element of power, we then considered how the balance of secrecy could be variably shifted between the Congress and the executive branch. We first determined that corruption may decrease an executive's claim to information. It was then established that serious requests for classified information might prove congressional needs for such materials. Finally, we noted that the judicial branch has played a limited role in changing the secrecy balance between the executive and the legislative branches of government.

BIBLIOGRAPHY

Aspin, Les and William Dickinson. Defense for a New Era: Lessons of the Persian Gulf War. Washington, D.C.: U.S. Government Printing Office, 1992.

Associated Press. "SDI Launch Failure Is Second in a Week." Washington Post, 28 October 1992, A17.

Associated Press. "SDI Rocket Destroyed in Flight." Washington Post, 24 October 1992, A7.

Associated Press. "U.S. Says Rocket Failed to Destroy Mock Warhead in Pacific Test." New York Times, 18 March 1992, B6.

Berger, Raoul. Executive Privilege: A Constitutional Myth. Cambridge, Massachusetts: Harvard University Press, 1974.

Beschloss, Michael R. The Crisis Years: Kennedy and Kruschev, 1960-1963. New York: Harper Collins Publishers, 1991.

Binkley, Wilfred Ellsworth. President and Congress. New York: Alfred A. Knopf, 1947.

Bishop, Joseph W., Jr. "The Executive Right of Privacy: An Unresolved Constitutional Question." Yale Law Journal 66 (1957): 484.

Bolte, Charles G. The Price for Peace: A Plan for Disarmament. Boston: The Beacon Press, 1956.

Borcherding, Katrin, Oleg I. Larichev and David M. Messick, ed. Contemporary Issues in Decision Making. New York: North-Holland, 1990.

Bowers, Claude G. Jefferson and Hamilton: The Struggle for Democracy in America. Cambridge, Massachusetts: The Riverside Press, 1925.

Boyd, Julian P. Number 7: Alexander Hamilton's Secret Attempt to Control American Foreign Policy. Princeton, New Jersey: Princeton University Press, 1964.

Broad, William J. "Serious Sharing of 'Star Wars?' Not in This Millennium." New York Times, February 23, 1992, Sect. 4, 5.

Broad, William J. Teller's War: The Top Secret Story Behind the Star Wars Deception. New York: Simon & Schuster, 1992.

Brzezinski, Zbigniew, Robert Jastrow, and Max M. Kampelman. "Defense in Space is Not 'Star Wars'." New York Times Magazine 27 Jan. 1985, late city final ed.: 28-29,46,48,51.

Bundy, McGeorge, et al. "The President's Choice: Star Wars or Arms Control." Foreign Affairs 63 (1984/1985): 264-278.

Bunn, Matthew. "GAO Reports Dispute Accuracy Of Missile Defense Claims." Arms Control Today, October 1992, 37.

Bunn, Matthew. "Pentagon Critique Delays 'Star Wars' Deployment." Arms Control Today, June 1992, 24.

Burrows, William E. Deep Black: Space Espionage and National Security. New York: Random House, 1986.

Carter, Ashton, John D. Steinbruner and Charles A. Zraket. Managing Nuclear Operations. Washington: Brookings Institution, 1987.

Carter, Ashton, and David N. Schwartz. Ballistic Missile Defense. Washington: Brookings Institution, 1984.

Carver, George A., Jr. "Intelligence in the Age of Glasnost." Foreign Affairs 69 (1990): 147-166.

Cline, Ray S. Secrets, Spies and Scholars: Blueprint of the Essential CIA. Washington, D.C.: Acropolis Books, 1976.

Cohn, Mary. Congressional Quarterly's Guide to Congress. 4th ed. Washington: Congressional Quarterly, 1991.

Cole, Jeff. "Defense Contractors Are Keeping the 'Star Wars' Program Alive." Wall Street Journal, 9 September 1992, B3.

Colton, David Everett. "Speaking Truth to Power: Intelligence Oversight in an Imperfect World." University of Pennsylvania Law Review 137 (1988): 571-613.

"Comment: United States v. A.T.&T.: Judicially Supervised Negotiation and Political Questions." Columbia Law Review 77 (1977): 466-494.

Cook, Nick. "GPALS Offer Slows UK Nuclear Plans." Jane's Defence Weekly, 4 July 1992, 9.

Cooper, Ambassador Henry F. "Congressional Misperceptions and the SDI Battle of the Budget." The Heritage Lectures, no. 408, Washington, D.C., 8 September 1992.

Crabb, Cecil V., Jr. and Pat M. Holt. Invitation to Struggle: Congress, the Presidency and Foreign Policy. Washington, D.C.: Congressional Quarterly Press, 1980.

Cushman, John H., Jr. "Whistleblower Wins Study of 'Star Wars' Program." New York Times, 3 March 1992, A13.

Dahl, Robert A. Congress and Foreign Policy. New York: Harcourt, Brace and Company, 1950.

Davidson, Paul. Controversies in Post Keynesian Economics. Brookfield, Vermont: Edward Elgar, 1991.

Demac, Donna A. Keeping America Uninformed: Government Secrecy in the 1980's. New York: Pilgrim Press, 1984.

"Developments in the Law-The National Security Interest and Civil Liberties." Harvard Law Review 85 (1972): 1130-1294.

DeVolpi, A. and others. Born Secret: The H-Bomb, The Progressive Case and National Security. New York: Pergamon Press, 1981.

Dixit, Avinash and Barry Nalebuff. Thinking Strategically: The Competitive Edge in Business, Politics and Everyday Life. New York: W.W. Norton, 1991.

Donovan, Robert J. Conflict and Crisis: The Presidency of Harry S. Truman, 1945-1948. New York: W.W. Norton & Company, 1977.

Edwards, George C., III, and Wallace Earl Walker, eds. National Security and the U.S. Constitution. Baltimore: Johns Hopkins University Press, 1988.

Evans, David. "Russian Urges U.S.: Make Weapons, Jobs." Chicago Tribune, 8 October 1992, Sect. 1., 4.

"Executive Privilege and the Congressional Right of Inquiry." Harvard Journal on Legislation 10 (1972): 621-671.

Farley, Philip J., Stephen S. Kaplan, and William H. Lewis. Arms Across the Sea. Washington: Brookings Institution, 1978.

Federyakov, Sergei. "Strategic Defence and Political Realities." International Affairs 3 (March 1992): 25-31.

Finnegan, Philip. "SDI Chief to Advise Veto if Congress Cuts Funds." Defense News, 14 September 1992, 4.

Finnegan, Philip. "SDI Impasse Threatens New Defense Projects." Defense News, 17-23 August 1992, 14.

Fleishman, Joel L., Lance Liebman, and Mark H. Moore, eds. Public Duties: The Moral Obligations of Government Officials. Cambridge, Massachusetts: Harvard University Press, 1981.

Ford Gerald R. A Time to Heal: The Autobiography of Gerald R. Ford. New York: Harper & Row Publishers, 1979.

"Ford Message to Rep. Pike on Contempt Issue." Congressional Quarterly Weekly Report, 29 November 1975, 2589-2590.

Frank Thomas M. and Michael J. Glennon. Foreign Relations and National Security Law: Cases, Materials and Simulations. Saint Paul, Minnesota: West Publishing, 1987.

Franck, Thomas M. and Edward Weisband, eds. Secrecy and Foreign Policy. New York: Oxford University Press, 1974.

Frantzich, Stephen E. Computers in Congress: The Politics of Information. Beverly Hills: Sage Publications, 1982.

Frazier, Howard, ed. Uncloaking the CIA. New York: The Free Press, 1975.

Fruend, Paul A. "The Supreme Court, 1973 Term: Foreword: On Presidential Privilege." Harvard Law Review 88 (1974): 13-39.

Furniss, Tim. "Small Packages." Flight International, 15 December 1992, 46-47.

Gaddis, John Lewis. The United States and the End of the Cold War: Implications, Reconsiderations, Provocations. New York: Oxford University Press, 1992.

Galnor, Itzhak, ed. Government Secrecy in Democracies. New York: New York University Press, 1977.

Gardner, Judy. "House: Pike Pushes Kissinger Contempt Citations." Congressional Quarterly Weekly Report 33 (1975): 2572.

Gilbert, Dennis A. Compendium of American Public Opinion. New York: Facts on File Publications, 1988.

Glynn, Patrick. Closing Pandora's Box: Arms Races, Arms Control, and the History of the Cold War. New York: Basic Books, 1992.

Gordon, Michael R. "'Star Wars X-Ray Laser Weapon Dies as Its Final Test Is Canceled." New York Times, 21 July 1992, A1, A16.

Granger, John V. Technology and International Relations. San Francisco: W.H. Freeman and Company, 1979.

Guide to American Law, 1984 ed., S.v. "Patents."

Guttman, Daniel and Barry Willner. The Shadow Government: The Government's Multi-Billion-Dollar Giveaway of Its Decision-Making Powers to Private Management Consultants, "Experts", and Think Tanks. New York: Pantheon Books, 1976.

Hackett, James. "Ignored by SDI Critics." Washington Times, 21 April 1992, F3.

Hackett, James. "SDI's Uncertain Future." Washington Times, 17 November 1992, F1 and F4.

Halperin, Morton H.. and Daniel N. Hoffman. Top Secret: National Security and the Right to Know. Washington, D.C.: New Republic Books, 1977.

Hamilton, Alexander, James Madison and John Jay. The Federalist. Cambridge, Massachusetts: Harvard University Press, 1961.

Hamilton, James and John C. Grabow. "Statute: A Legislative Proposal Resolving Executive Privilege Disputes Precipitated By Congressional Subpoenas." Harvard Journal of Legislation 21 (1984): 145-172.

Hamilton, James. The Power to Probe: A Study of Congressional Investigations. New York: Random House, 1976.

Heise, Juergen Arthur. Minimum Disclosure: How the Pentagon Manipulates the News. New York: W.W. Norton, 1979.

Henderson, Breck W. "SDIO Opts for Balloon Testing To Support Directed Energy Plans." Aviation Week and Space Technology, 27 July 1992, 58-59.

Henderson, Breck W. "SDIO Planning Mission With Russian Topaz 2 Reactor." Aviation Week and Space Technology, 29 July 1992, 57-58.

Hitshleifer, Jack. The Analytics of Uncertainty and Information. New York: Cambridge University Press, 1992.

Hirshleifer, Jack. Time, Uncertainty and Information. New York: Basil Blackwell, 1989.

Hutchings, Raymond. Soviet Secrecy and Non-Secrecy. Totowa, New Jersey: Barnes & Noble Books, 1988.

Isaacson, Walter. Kissinger: A Biography. New York: Simon & Schuster, 1992.

Jastrow, Robert and Max M. Kampelman. "Why We Still Need SDI." Commentary, 94 (November 1992): 23-29.

Jefferson, Thomas. The Writings of Thomas Jefferson, Vol. I. Andrew A. Lipscomb, ed. Washington, D.C.: The Thomas Jefferson Memorial Association, 1904.

Johnson, Loch K. A Season of Inquiry: The Senate Intelligence Investigation. Lexington: University of Kentucky Press, 1985.

Kaplan, David A. "A Safety Net Full of Holes." Newsweek, 23 March 1992, 56-57, 59.

Kapstein, Ethan Barnaby. The Political Economy of National Security: A Global Perspective. New York: McGraw-Hill, 1992.

"Keeping Secrets: Congress, The Courts and National Security Information." Harvard Law Review 103 (1990): 906-925.

Kennedy, Paul. Preparing for the Twenty-First Century. New York: Random House, 1993.

Kennedy, Paul. The Rise and Fall of the Great Powers: Economic Change and Military Conflict from 1500 to 2000. New York: Random House, 1987.

Kiernan, Vincent. "Simulations Change SDI Thinking." Space News, 20 April 1992, 7.

King, Anthony, ed. The New American Political System. Washington, D.C.: American Enterprise Institute, 1978.

Kingdon, John W. Congressional Voting Decisions. 3rd ed. Ann Arbor: University of Michigan Press, 1989.

Kirzner, Israel M. Discovery, Capitalism, and Distributive Justice. New York: Basil Blackwell, 1989.

Kissinger, Henry A. Nuclear Weapons and Foreign Policy. New York: Harper & Brothers, 1957.

Koh, Harold Hongju. The National Security Constitution: Sharing Power after the Iran Contra Affair. New Haven, Connecticut: Yale University Press, 1990.

Kosminsky, Jay P., ed. "SDI Issues Update." The SDI Report, 15 January 1992, 1-2.

Kosminsky, Jay P., ed. "SDI Issues Update." The SDI Report, 20 February 1992, 1-2.

Krehbiel, Keith. Information and Legislative Organization. Ann Arbor: University of Michigan Press, 1991.

Lardner, George. "Cheney Told to Probe Scientist's Charge of Misconduct, Waste by SDI Officials." Washington Post, 2 March 1992, A5.

Lardner, George. "Pryor Says SDI Is Tainted by Contractors." Washington Post, 28 February 1992, A21.

Lardner, George. "SDI Scientist Wins Reprieve From Firing." Washington Post, 7 March 1992, A8.

Lardner, George. "'Star Wars' Plan Invites Problems, GAO Warns." Washington Post, 11 March 1992, A7.

Laurance, Edward J. The International Arms Trade. New York: Lexington Books, 1992.

Lawler, Andrew. "SDI Inquiry Targets Space Data." Space News, 2 November 1992, 1, 28.

Lazo, Rodrigo. "Whistleblower Fired From Star Wars Staff." Federal Times, 2 March 1992, 5.

Levy, David M. The Economic Ideas of Ordinary People. New York: Routledge, 1992.

Lewy, Guenter "Can Democracy Keep Secrets? Do We Need an Official Secrets Act?" Policy Review 26 (Fall 1983): 17-29.

Lewis, Flora. "It's Lunacy to Keep 'Star Wars' Alive." New York Times, 22 February 1992, 23.

Loewenheim, Francis L., Harold D. Langley and Manfred Jonas. Roosevelt and Churchill: The Secret Wartime Correspondence. New York: E.P. Dutton & Company, 1975.

Lord, Carnes. The Presidency and the Management of National Security. New York: The Free Press, 1988.

Mainuddin, Rolin G. "SDI: The Impact on Deterrence." Military Review 72 (March 1992): 60-65.

March, James G. Decisions and Organizations. New York: Basil Blackwell, 1988.

Maxwell, Elliot E "The CIA's Secret Funding and the Constitution." Yale Law Journal 84 (1975): 608-636.

McCall, John J., ed. The Economics of Information and Uncertainty. Chicago: University of Chicago Press, 1982.

McKenna, C.J. The Economics of Uncertainty. New York: Oxford University Press, 1986.

McNamara, Robert S. Out of the Cold: New Thinking for American Foreign and Defense Policy in the 21st Century. New York: Simon and Schuster, 1989.

Meeks, J. Gay Tulip, ed. Thoughtful Economic Man: Essays on Rationality, Moral Rules and Benevolence. New York: Cambridge University Press, 1991.

Miller, Nathan. Spying For America: The Hidden History of U.S. Intelligence. New York: Paragon House, 1989.

Morrison, David C. "Dancing in the Dark." National Journal, 11 April 1987: 867-873.

Morrison, David C. "Missile Defenses: More Debate." National Journal, 8 February 1992: 337-339.

Morrison, David C. "Tilting with Intelligence." National Journal, 9 May 1987: 1110-1115.

Mullen, John D. and Byron M. Roth. _Decision Making: It's Logic and Practice_. Savage, Maryland: Rowman and Littlefield Publishers, 1991.

Nessen, Ron. _It Sure Looks Different from the Inside_. New York: Simon and Schuster, 1978.

Nieburg, Harold L. _Nuclear Secrecy and Foreign Policy_. Washington: Public Affairs Press, 1964.

Niemi, Richard G., John Mueller and Tom W. Smith. _Trends in Public Opinion: A Compendium of Survey Data_. New York: Greenwood Press, 1989.

Nye, Joseph S., Jr., and James A. Schear, eds. _Seeking Stability in Space: Anti-Satellite Weapons and the Evolving Space Regime_. Lanham, Maryland: University Press of America, 1987.

Opall, Barbara. "U.S. Scientists Urge Shift in SDI Direction." _Defense News_, 4 May 1992, 35.

Oseth, John M. _Regulating U.S. Intelligence Operations: A Study in Definition of the National Interest_. Lexington, Kentucky: University Press of Kentucky, 1985.

Pascall, Glenn R. and Robert D. Lamson. _Guns & Butter: Recapturing America's Momentum After a Military Decade_. Washington: Macmillan Publishing, 1991.

Peck, Merton J. and Frederic M. Scherer. _The Weapons Acquisition Process: An Economic Analysis_. Boston: Harvard University Graduate School of Business Administration, 1962.

Persico, Joseph E. _Casey: From the OSS to the CIA_. New York: Penguin Books, 1990.

Pfaltzgraff, Robert L. and Jacquelyn K. Davis. _National Security Decisions: The Participants Speak_. Lexington, Massachusetts: Lexington Books, 1990.

Phlips, Louis. _The Economics of Imperfect Information_. New York: Cambridge University Press, 1988.

"Pike Committee: Kissinger Contempt Citation." _Congressional Quarterly Weekly Report_ 33 (1975): 2506.

Polmar, Norman. The Ships and Aircraft of the U.S. Fleet,
     14th ed. Annapolis, Maryland: Naval Institute Press,
     1987.

Relyea, Harold C., et al. The Presidency and Information
     Policy. Vol. 4. New York: Center for the Study of the
     Presidency. 4 vols. 1981.

Robins, Kevin, ed. Understanding Information: Business,
     Technology and Geography. London: Belhaven Press,
     1992.

Robinson, William H. and Clay H. Wellborn, eds. Knowledge,
     Power and the Congress. Washington, D.C.: Congressional
     Quarterly, 1991.

Rogers, David and Thomas E. Ricks. "Senate Approves $3.8
     Billion Funds For SDI Program." Wall Street Journal, 18
     September 1992, A7.

Rosenthal, Paul C. and Robert S. Grossman. "Congressional
     Access to Confidential Information Collected by Federal
     Agencies." Harvard Journal on Legislation 15 (1977):
     74-118.

Ross, Andrew L., ed. The Political Economy of National
     Defense: Issues and Perspectives. New York: Greenwood
     Press, 1991.

Rudney, Dr. Robert. "GPALS and the NATO Allies." Strategic
     Review, 20 (Summer 1992): 69-75.

Rudney, Dr. Robert. "GPALS Tempts Israel to Abandon
     Offensive Stance." Armed Forces Journal International,
     February 1992 42-43.

Ruina, Jack. "Edward Teller and the Folly Of Star Wars."
     Arms Control Today, May 1992, 29-30.

Saucier, Aldric. "Lost in Space." New York Times, 9 March
     1992, A17.

Savelyev, Alexander. "Toward U.S.-Russian Strategic Defense:
     Ban the ABM Treaty Now." Heritage Foundation
     Backgrounder. 12 November 1992, 1-2.

Schmergel, Greg, ed. U.S. Foreign Policy in the 1990's. New
     York: Saint Martin's Press, 1991.

Schmitt, Eric. "Democratic Senators Challenging Cost and Risk of 'Star Wars' Plan." New York Times, 10 April 1992, A25.

Schudson, Michael. Watergate in American Memory: How We Remember, Forget, and Reconstruct the Past. New York: Basic Books, 1992.

Smist, Frank J. Congress Oversees the United States Intelligence Community, 1947-1989. Knoxville: University of Tennessee Press, 1990.

Smith, R. Jeffrey. "SDI Adopts 'High Risk' Procurement." Washington Post, 3 July 1992, A6.

Smith, R. Jeffrey. "SDI Success Said to Be Overstated." Washington Post, 16 September 1992, A1, A18.

Smith, Steven S., and Christopher J. Deering. Committees in Congress. 2nd ed. Washington: Congressional Quarterly Press, 1990.

Sowell, Thomas. Knowledge and Decisions. New York: Basic Books, 1980.

Spring, Baker. "The Senate Armed Services Committee's About Face on the Missile Defense Act." Heritage Foundation Executive Memorandum, 5 August 1992, 1-2.

Staniland, Martin. What is Political Economy? A Study of Social Theory and Underdevelopment. New Haven, Connecticut: Yale University Press, 1985.

Starr, Barbara. "Make or Break for SDI as ABM Doubts Surface." Janes Defence Weekly, 4 July 1992, 15.

Starr, Barbara. "SDI Funds Sought for Aegis Ships." Jane's Defence Weekly, 21 November 1992, 13.

Stein, Arthur A. Why Nations Cooperate: Circumstances and Choice in International Relations. Ithaca, New York: Cornell University Press, 1990.

Tirman, John. Sovereign Acts: American Unilateralism and Global Security. New York: Harper & Row Publishers, 1989.

Towell, Pat. "Anti-Missile Coalition Is Divided On Space vs. Ground Defense." Congressional Quarterly Weekly Report, 23 May 1992, 1461-1462.

Towell, Pat. "Critics Score Points Against SDI As Weapons Debate Begins." <u>Congressional Quarterly Weekly Report</u>, 8 August 1992, 2375-2381.

Towell, Pat. "Senate Bill Avoids Showdown With $3.8 Billion for SDI." <u>Congressional Quarterly Weekly Report</u>, 19 September 1992, 2831-2832.

Uhlmann, Jeffery K. "Algorithms for Multiple-Target Tracking." <u>American Scientist</u> 80 (March-April 1992): 128-141.

U.S. Congress. House. Committee on Foreign Affairs. <u>The War Powers Resolution: A Special Study of the Committee on Foreign Affairs</u>. Committee Print. 97th Cong., 2d Sess. Washington, D.C.: GPO, 1982.

U.S. Congress. House. Committee on Government Operations. <u>A Citizen's Guide on Using the Freedom of Information Act and the Privacy Act of 1974 to Request Government Records</u>. Report. 102d Cong., 1st Sess. Washington, D.C.: GPO, 1991.

U.S. Congress. House. Committee on Government Operations. <u>Presidential Directives and Records Accountability Act</u>. Hearing on H.R. 5092. 100th Cong., 2d Sess. Washington, D.C.: GPO, 1989.

U.S. Congress. House. Committee on Public Works and Transportation. <u>Contempt of Congress</u>. Report. 97th Cong., 2d Sess. Washington, D.C.: G.P.O., 1982.

U.S. Congress. House. Investigations Subcommittee of the Committee on Armed Services. <u>NATO/MOUs</u>. 102nd Cong., 2nd Sess. Washington, D.C.: G.P.O., 1992.

U.S. Congress. House. Permanent Select Committee on Intelligence. <u>Compilation of Intelligence Laws and Related Laws and Executive Orders of Interest to the National Intelligence Community</u>. Committee print. 101st Cong., 2nd Sess. Washington, D.C.: G.P.O., 1990.

U.S. Congress. House. Subcommittee of the Committee on Government Operations. <u>Availability of Information to Congress</u>. 95th Cong., 1st Sess. H.R. Res. 4938, 5983, 6438. Washington: GPO, 1973.

U.S. Congress. House. Subcommittee on Arms Control, International Security and Science of the Committee on Foreign Affairs. <u>U.S. Military Sales and Assistance Programs: Laws, Regulations, and Procedures</u>. 99th Cong., 1st Sess. Washington, D.C.: G.P.O., 1985.

U.S. Congress. Joint Committee on Congressional Operations.
<u>Leading Cases on Congressional Investigatory Power</u>.
94th Cong., 2d Sess. Washington, D.C.: G.P.O., 1976.

U.S. Congress. Senate. Committee on Foreign Relations.
<u>Nomination of Richard Helms to be Ambassador to Iran
and CIA International and Domestic Activities</u>. 93rd
Cong., 1st Sess. Washington, D.C.: G.P.O., 1974.

U.S. Congress. Senate. Select Committee on Intelligence.
<u>Annual Report to the Senate</u>. Committee print. 95th
Cong., 1st Sess. Washington, D.C.: G.P.O., 1977.

U.S. Congress. Senate. Subcommittee on Constitutional Rights
of the Committee on the Judiciary. <u>The Power of the
President to Withhold Information from the Congress:
Memorandums of the Attorney General</u>. 85th Cong., 2nd
Sess. Washington: G.P.O., 1958.

U.S. Library of Congress. Congressional Research Service.
<u>Access to Government Information in the United States</u>,
by Harold C. Relyea. September 25, 1991. CRS Report 91-
697 GOV.

U.S. Library of Congress. Congressional Research Service.
<u>The Application of the Freedom of Information Act to
Congress: A Legal Analysis</u>, by Jay Shampansky. April
28, 1992. CRS Report 92-403 A.

U.S. Library of Congress. Congressional Research Service.
<u>Congressional Access To Information From the
Executive:A Legal Analysis</u>, by Richard Ehlke. March 10,
1986. CRS Report 86-50 A.

U.S. Library of Congress. Congressional Research Service.
<u>Export Controls</u>, by Glennon J. Harrison and George
Holliday. March 2, 1993. CRS Issue Brief 91064.

U.S. Library of Congress. Congressional Research Service.
<u>Legal Issues Related to the Possible Release of
Classified Information by Senators, Representatives or
Members of Their Staffs</u>, by Elizabeth B. Bazan. May 22,
1989. CRS Report 89-322A.

U.S. Library of Congress. Congressional Research Service.
<u>Missile Proliferation: A Discussion of U.S. Objectives
and Policy Options</u>, by Robert Shuey. February 21, 1990.
CRS Report 90-120F.

U.S. Library of Congress. Congressional Research Service.
<u>Nuclear Arms Control After START</u>, by Amy Woolf. March
5, 1993. CRS Issue Brief 91148.

U.S. Library of Congress. Congressional Research Service. War Powers Resolution: Presidential Compliance, by Ellen C. Collier. January 14, 1993. CRS Issue Brief 81050.

U.S. President. Public Papers of the Presidents of the United States. Washington, D.C.: Office of the Federal Register, National Archives and Records Service, 1974-. Gerald R. Ford, 1975.

Weida, William J. and Frank L. Gertcher. The Political Economy of National Defense. Boulder, Colorado: Westview Press, 1987.

Weiner, Tim. Blank Check: The Pentagon's Black Budget. New York: Warner Books, 1990.

Wellborn, Stan, Public Affairs Director, The Brookings Institution. Interview by author, 11 March 1993, Washington, D.C., Transcript.

Westin, Alan F., ed. Information Technology in a Democracy. Cambridge, Massachusetts: Harvard University Press, 1971.

Wirls, Daniel. Buildup: The Politics of Defense in the Reagan Era. Ithaca, New York: Cornell University Press, 1992.

Wu, Silas H.L. Communication and Imperial Control in China: Evolution of the Palace Memorial System, 1693-1735. Cambridge, Massachusetts: Harvard University Press, 1970.

Zacharias, Ellis M. Behind Closed Doors: The Secret History of the Cold War. New York: G.P. Putnam's Sons, 1950.

www.ingramcontent.com/pod-product-compliance
Lightning Source LLC
Chambersburg PA
CBHW081354280526
45788CB00009B/2881